Proceedings of the

19th International Congress of Classical Archaeology

Volume 6: The Riverlands of Aegean Thrace /

River Valleys and Regional Economies

Proceedings of the
19th International Congress of Classical Archaeology

Cologne/Bonn, 22 – 26 May 2018
Archaeology and Economy in the Ancient World

Edited by

Martin Bentz and Michael Heinzelmann

Volume 6

ICCA
XIX
AIAC

Edited by

Eurydice Kefalidou

A. The Riverlands of Aegean Thrace: Production, Consumption and Exploitation of the Natural and Cultural Landscapes
B. River Valleys and Regional Economies

Panel 2.4 / 2.7

Propylaeum
SPECIALIZED INFORMATION
SERVICE CLASSICS

Bibliographic information published by the Deutsche Nationalbibliothek:
The Deutsche Nationalbibliothek lists this publication in the Deutsche Nationalbibliografie; detailed bibliographic data are available on the Internet at http://dnb.dnb.de.

Propylaeum
SPECIALIZED INFORMATION SERVICE CLASSICS

Published at Propylaeum,
Heidelberg University Library 2022.

This publication is freely available under https://www.propylaeum.de (Open Access).
URN: urn:nbn:de:bsz:16-propylaeum-ebook-871-6
DOI: https://doi.org/10.11588/propylaeum.871

Editorial Coordination: Florian Birkner, Ina Borkenstein, Christian Schöne
Editorial Staff: Stefanie Herten, Katharina Zerzeropulos

Layout: Torsten Zimmer, Zwiebelfisch@quarium

Cover illustration: Valley of the River Nestos in Aegean Thrace
(© Ephorate of Antiquitites of Xanthi – Digital Editing: Nina Baka)

ISBN: 978-3-96929-056-9
e-ISBN: 978-3-96929-055-2

Universität zu Köln

UNIVERSITÄT BONN

CONTENTS

B. River Valleys and Regional Economies

PREFACE

On behalf of the 'Associazione Internazionale di Archeologia Classica (AIAC)' the 19th International Congress for Classical Archaeology took place in Cologne and Bonn from 22 to 26 May 2018. It was jointly organized by the two Archaeological Institutes of the Universities of Cologne and Bonn, and the primary theme of the congress was 'Archaeology and Economy in the Ancient World'. In fact, economic aspects permeate all areas of public and private life in ancient societies, whether in urban development, religion, art, housing, or in death.

Research on ancient economies has long played a significant role in ancient history. Increasingly in the last decades, awareness has grown in archaeology that the material culture of ancient societies offers excellent opportunities for studying the structure, performance, and dynamics of ancient economic systems and economic processes. Therefore, the main objective of this congress was to understand economy as a central element of classical societies and to analyze its interaction with ecological, political, social, religious, and cultural factors. The theme of the congress was addressed to all disciplines that deal with the Greco-Roman civilization and their neighbouring cultures from the Aegean Bronze Age to the end of Late Antiquity.

The participation of more than 1.200 scholars from more than 40 countries demonstrates the great response to the topic of the congress. Altogether, more than 900 papers in 128 panels were presented, as were more than 110 posters. The publication of the congress is in two stages: larger panels are initially presented as independent volumes, such as this publication. Finally, at the end of the editing process, all contributions will be published in a joint conference volume.

We would like to take this opportunity to thank all participants and helpers of the congress who made it such a great success. Its realization would not have been possible without the generous support of many institutions, whom we would like to thank once again: the Universities of Bonn and Cologne, the Archaeological Society of Cologne, the Archaeology Foundation of Cologne, the Gerda Henkel Foundation, the Fritz Thyssen Foundation, the Sal. Oppenheim Foundation, the German Research Foundation (DFG), the German Academic Exchange Service (DAAD), the Romano-Germanic Museum Cologne and the LVR-LandesMuseum Bonn. Finally, our thanks go to all colleagues and panel organizers who were involved in the editing and printing process.

Bonn/Cologne, in August 2019

Martin Bentz & Michael Heinzelmann

2.4 / 2.7 Introduction

Eurydice Kefalidou

For both the archaeologist and the native dweller,
the landscape tells – or rather is – a story.
It enfolds the lives and times of predecessors who,
over the generations, have moved around in it
and played their part in its formation.
To perceive the landscape is therefore
to carry out an act of remembrance,
and remembering is not so much
a matter of calling up an internal image, stored in the mind,
as of engaging perceptually with an environment
that is itself pregnant with the past.

Tim Ingold, The Temporality of the Landscape, 1993

I am grateful to the AIAC 2018 Organizing Committee for the invitation to organize and edit Panel 2.4, and to edit Panel 2.7 since they both explore multiple facets of economic activity in Central and Eastern Mediterranean riverlands and river deltas. My warmest thanks to all my colleagues who presented original studies, contributed in thought-provoking discussions both during and after the conference, and submitted their papers and extended summaries timely for publication.

A. The Riverlands of Aegean Thrace: Production, Consumption and Exploitation of the Natural and Cultural Landscapes

The Riverlands of Aegean Thrace: Production, Consumption and Exploitation of the Natural and Cultural Landscapes – An Overview

Eurydice Kefalidou

Macedonia and Thrace are considered as the 'river-and-lake districts' of Greece. Large rivers and lakes, most of which keep their names since antiquity, define the geography and the history of the settlements which develop near them.

The papers of this section elucidate the natural and cultural character of the river lands of Aegean Thrace, i.e. the northeast part of Greece and the European part of Turkey. Herodotos (VII. 59, 108–109) is the first ancient writer who in the 5th c. BC made an extensive reference to the rivers and lakes of the area, while describing the march of Xerxes' army in 480 BC: "The territory of Doriskos is in Thrace, a wide plain by the sea, and through it flows a great river, the Evros; here had been built that royal fortress which is called Doriskos, and a Persian guard had been posted there by Darius ever since the time of his march against Scythia... On his [i.e.Xerxes] road from Doriskos he first passed the Samothracian fortresses of these, the city built farthest to the west is called Mesambria. Next to it is the Thasian city of Stryme; between them runs the river Lissos, which now could not furnish water enough for Xerxes' army, but was exhausted... After he had crossed the dried-up bed of the river Lisos, he passed by the Greek cities of Maroneia, Dikaia, and Abdera. He passed by these, and along certain well-known lakes near them: the Ismaris lake that lies between Maroneia and Stryme, and near Dikaia the Vistonis lake into which the rivers Travos and Kompsatos discharge. Near Abdera Xerxes passed no well-known lake, but crossed the river Nestos where it flows into the sea..." (my italics – cf. also Herodotos IV.90: "...the Evros, which empties into the sea near the city of Ainos").

Almost all rivers of the Aegean Thrace run from north to south, i.e. from the Rhodopi mountain range via the fertile coastal Thracian plain to the Aegean Sea or to Lake Vistonis. Their gradually and constantly altering routes, deltas, marshlands, wetlands, dunes and lagoons form a rather complex natural environment, which influenced all aspects of life in antiquity, in both positive and negative ways.

For the most part these rivers were vital supports for people and economies. They provided water for people and animals, irrigated the land, facilitated trade and commerce through small vessels or rafts, aided industrial activities, formed a rich area for fishermen and hunters, and offered raw materials such as sand and gravel. At the same time, their deltas and marshlands, especially in periods of flood, created an inhospitable environment, often unsuitable for habitation, causing illnesses like malaria that affected the local population in a variety of ways. Furthermore, these rivers connected the sea and the littoral zone with the hinterland, and thus they allowed the interaction between the Greek colonies on the Aegean coast with the local Thracian tribes, which inhabited the inland part of this region.

Recent research in Aegean Thrace includes two systematic surveys in the deltas of the Nestos and the Lissos (papers by C. Kallintzi et al., and N. Arrington et al.), a rescue excavation in the city of Doriskos near Evros (extensive summary by Ch. Karadima), a project on the harbor city of Ainos on the Evros delta (extensive summary by T. Schmidts) and a project utilizing spatial technology along river courses (paper by D. Tsiafaki and V. Evangelidis). These projects adopt a variety of approaches and methodologies: collecting and studying archaeological material, utilizing satellite images, conducting geophysical surveys, employing geoarchaeology and geoinformatics, etc. They all aim at defining the character of various ancient riverside sites, integrating them into their broader landscape and understanding aspects of exploitation, production, consumption, communication and trade.

The aim of this panel was to bring together experts working in both Greece and Turkey in order to address topics such as (among others) the reconfiguration of ancient river routes and the settlement patterns that were formed around them; the various uses of land and the means of exploitation through time; the boundaries of the *chora* of various cities, towns, villages and farmsteads; the density of population in various landscape settings and the movements of (or tensions between) different groups that moved or expanded beyond their original habitation zone due to environmental and/or economic reasons.

Archaic and Classical Abdera: Economy and Wealth by the Nestos Riverside

Constantina Kallintzi – Merkouris Georgiadis – Eurydice Kefalidou – Kyriaki Chatziprokopiou

The City

Abdera was founded in the broader context of the colonization of Aegean Thrace during the Archaic period as a colony of two neighbouring coastal Ionian cities, successively: Clazomenae (mid 7th century BC) and Teos (mid 6th century BC).[1] The selection of this particular site was dictated by economic factors, since the area was rich in metals, timber and horses, its fertile plains were ideal for the cultivation of vines and cereals as well as for animal breeding, especially cattle and sheep, and finally, it was easy to obtain slaves from the Thracian hinterland.[2] Moreover, the site had a gulf protected from the winds and the privilege of being near to the then outfall of river Nestos and to the end of the land passageways leading to the hinterland. The early habitation site ("North Enclosure") is ca 1 km^2 in size, and protected by a large fortification wall (fig. 1-A).[3]

Political factors played an important role for the second wave of colonisers because the Teians left their homeland due to the Persian expansionism. One of the first things they did was remodelling the fortification walls along the route of the earlier wall (with some modifications), emphasising the importance of security against the Thracians. In the last quarter of the 6th century BC a sanctuary just outside the walls, possibly dedicated to Demeter and Kore,[4] was elaborated with a monumental staircase and probably a building (fig. 1-B). This type of monumentalisation reveals the economic success of the Teians already from their first generation. In the same period a shipshed, specialised for warships, was constructed at the northeast edge of the harbour, parallel to the city wall at a distance of 6 m (fig. 1-C).[5]

During the Megabazos' campaign in 512–510 BC[6] Abdera came under the Persian rule that lasted until 476/475 BC. The port of Abdera acted as a base of the Persian fleet, while in 479 BC the city of Abdera had the economic capability to host Xerxes and his large army.[7] Soon afterwards, an enormous supply of clastic sediments from river Nestos was observed in the port facilities suggesting that a process of port silting was under way.[8] A strong water break has been constructed in the mid 5th century BC; large unworked boulders of granite were employed probably coming from the northern part of Xanthi and the Rhodopi mountains; moreover, two main local sandstone (psammite) quarries were also used in this period (fig. 2).[9]

For the rest of the 5th century BC Abdera was allied to Athens and became democratic regarding its political system.[10] The list of the Delian League members (last quarter of the 5th century BC) shows that Abdera paid the second highest tax to the alliance thus suggesting the particular wealth of the city.[11] However, the Abderitans were always at

Fig. 1: Abdera: The Sanctuary of Demeter (B), the city walls (A) and the shipshed (C).

the mercy of environmental changes caused mainly by the Nestos river delta, which finally turned the entire gulf into marshland by the mid 4th century BC. Consequently, at the late 4th / early 3rd century BC the initial site was abandoned and the city was transferred in the so called 'South Enclosure',[12] where a new harbour was constructed.

The evidence discussed here combines old and new data, the latter stemming from a new period of research for the city of Abdera and the Xanthi District that began in 2015. The "Archaeological Project at Abdera and Xanthi (APAX)" aims to study the city and *chora* of Abdera in its regional context. The expedition is a cooperation between the Xanthi Ephorate of Antiquities, Prof. E. Kefalidou (National and Kapodistrian University of Athens), Dr. M. Georgiadis (Catalan Institute of Classical Archaeology), and specialists from Greek and foreign universities.[13]

The Surrounding Area: Farmsteads and Graveyards

Despite the tension between Greek colonists and the indigenous Thracians from time to time, which are reported by ancient written sources, farmsteads were established outside the city walls.[14] This phenomenon appears already in the early 5th century BC in accordance to similar examples from southern Greek *poleis*. A new concept of exploiting

Fig. 2: Abdera: A local sandstone (psammite) quarry.

the landscape and its resources, the ancient *chora*, was preferred during the Classical period. There is a discussion whether these structures acted as permanent habitation sites or not, but the remains (storage pithoi, amphoras, loom weights, grinding stones, etc.) suggest that household production was taking place there, while the presence of slags argues that, at least occasionally, industrial activities happened there. The farmsteads show that a new economic model was opted for exploiting the land and processing the agro-silvo-pastoral produce closer to their production area.

The greatest enemies of the first settlers, the Clazomenians, were the poor climatic conditions caused by the marshlands. The majority of early graves, situated very close to the city wall, consisted of amphora and pithos burials, few of which had burial offerings, mainly pottery, both local and imported (Corinthian and east Greek wares).[15] The relatively 'poor' grave offerings, keeping in mind that ca. 80% of the graves belonged to infants and young children, throw some light not only on burial practices but also on the level of wealth in the colony. Physical anthropology analyses demonstrated that people's diet consisted mainly of fish and secondarily of vegetables.[16] The adult skeletons suffered from vitamin C deficiency and both genders performed heavy labour. Many infants and children suffered from anaemia, scurvy

Fig. 3: *Chora* of Abdera: Two burial tumuli.

and childhood diseases, many of which can be connected with slow moving and often stagnant water and an environment full of marshland, an ideal context for transmitting malaria. The animal bones recovered belong mainly to sheep, goats and bovines. The latter along with horse bones provide an insight of the animals employed for traction in agricultural works.

The evidence from mid 6th century BC onwards graves suggests the introduction of new burial customs probably due to the Teian colonists.[17] Tumuli were erected and contained a number of graves, often for several generations (fig. 3). These significantly altered the flat, river and marshland landscape to one with many man-made hills visible to everyone. The bodies of the deceased were placed in terracotta or stone sarcophagi made out of sandstone. The sarcophagi were well-worked, heavy and expensive objects, which come into contrast to the limited rich burial offerings. Pottery, both local and imported, is the commonest offering. Thus, in the burial practices of this period the demonstration of wealth was low perhaps associated with the Teian burial customs or/and the democratic ethos of the 5th century BC rather than the degree of economic power of the *polis.*

On the contrary, during the 4th and early 3rd century BC 22% of the graves contained jewellery.[18] In this period one third of the graves with jewellery included gold ones, revealing that wealth was clearly demonstrated within the burial practices. The *polis* may have become richer and/or it was easier to show the wealth of the individual more freely than before. Philip II and the Macedonian rule may have provided more peaceful conditions, in which the city thrived as indicated by the striking of the first gold coins in the second half of the 4th century BC, as we will see next.

Fig. 4: Silver and bronze coinage of Abdera.

Other Evidence for Economy and Wealth

Metal and coinage

Abdera gained access to metal sources early on. These sources are not located east of Nestos River, but in the area between the rivers Nestos and Strymon, which was under the control of Thasos that acted as a competitor to Abdera. Thus, it can be deduced that the metal source related to Abdera was situated in the hinterland of Thrace, with which a close interaction had been established as the written sources reveal. These ties are highlighted by the acceptance of Nymphodoros of Abdera in the royal family of Sitalke, king of the Odryssians.[19]

Numerous metal slags were recovered in the northwestern and central-northern part of the *polis*, suggesting that iron was worked systematically in this region, while at least one kiln for producing bronze has been excavated as well.[20] This and other kilns could have been used for the minting of silver and gold coins. Moreover, some pieces of iron came straight from the iron ore demonstrating that some primary stages of metal production took place in the city.

The rapid beginning of the Abderite coinage already from the last quarter of the 5th century BC with heavy weight issues of octodrachms and tetradrachms suggests that the Teians established an important network of commercial contacts with the Thracians or/and the Thasians, who controlled the silver-bearing region and could

Fig. 5: Abdera: APAX survey: Relief terracotta sarcophagi (left) and architectural terracottas (right).

supply the colonists with the metal necessary for their monetary issues (fig. 4). The approximately seven centuries of its coinage (520/515 BC until the reign of Antoninus Pius, 138–161 AD) are divided into 14 periods, including silver, gold and bronze issues. During the first seven periods of the mint the city adopted different monetary standards, simultaneously in use: one for the silver coins of high intrinsic value (octodrachms and tetradrachms) destined for international commerce and one for the small denominations (drachms, tetrobols, triobols, obols and hemi-obols) destined for local transactions.[21] The civic numismatic iconography is characterised by an exquisite artistic quality and by a big variety on reverse types in contrast to the obverse, which almost always bears the main numismatic type, a griffin to the left.

The iconography of Abderite coinage draws on the city's religious cults, its geography and local products. Dionysos, the patron deity of the city and his attributes (kantharos, cup, krater, grape-cluster and ivy-leaf) imply the veneration of the god and emphasise the local wine production. The cultivation of grain in this "bountiful land" is represented by ears of corn on some coins of the sixth period (395–360 BC). Marine creatures like dolphins, tunas and seashells indicate the impact of the sea on Abderitan economic and everyday life. Finally, the depiction of horses, rams, bulls and goats refers the importance of livestock farming.[22]

In conclusion: metal industry appears to be an important element of the local economy, and the river Nestos could have provided the necessary route for the dissemination of metals from their mountain sources to the port of Abdera and the Aegean.

Fig. 6: Abdera: APAX survey: Pottery fragments.

Architectural Terracottas

Many fragments of relief antefixes, mainly of the palmettes-and-spirals type, and a few parts of relief simai, sometimes painted with various colours, have been found in certain parts of the city (fig. 5-right). The few simai could have belonged to public buildings but many of the antefixes can be connected with habitation areas. This type of embellishment may look peculiar for the private houses, which were constructed mainly by unworked stones and only a few worked sandstones have been recovered mainly as door frames.[23] Although their analysis is in a preliminary stage,[24] the use of ornate antefixes in the domestic architecture could have been an indication of economic success and wealth in the local society, or at least in some of its members, from the late Archaic period onwards.

Pottery and Terracotta Production

The clay of most architectural terracottas, as well as their recurring ornaments, point towards a local production for many of these artefacts. The same is true for the largest part of pottery from the city and its graveyards, plain, relief and painted (fig. 6). Of particular interest is the relief ware, mostly dated to the late Archaic and early Classical periods It is characterised by different shapes including louteria, perirrhanteria, stands, pithoi and deep bowls. Terracotta relief sarcophagi display close stylistic similarities with relief vases and were probably produced in the same workshops (fig. 5-left)[25].

Fig. 7: Abdera: APAX survey: Stamped handles of transport amphoras.

Moreover, remains of clay kilns have been noted close to the port in the northwestern part of the city, as well as to the north end close to the city walls. These areas could have acted as industrial areas within the city, which certainly produced a variety of objects, including transport amphoras discussed next.[26]

Transport Amphoras

Transport amphoras are a good indicator of economy regarding the production, storage and import/export of goods in a site. The detailed study of the amphoras from the 'North Enclosure' is in process (fig. 7).[27] Imported transport amphoras help to map out the intensity of trade that Abdera conducted with the world beyond it. About 80% of them has northern Aegean provenance, i.e. from the Chalcidice peninsula to the west up to the Dardanelles to the east. The commercial contacts extended at least occasionally as far as Heracleia Pontica and Sinope in the Black Sea. Large numbers (20%) come also from the east Aegean, where the two *metropoleis* of the city were located and as far south as Rhodes. Of great importance is the fact that there is strong evidence for a local transport amphora production of the 5th and 4th centuries BC, thus suggesting that there was a significant production of agro-silvo-pastoral goods. Moreover, the high concentration of transport amphoras in the northwestern end of the city may suggest the existence of storage buildings by the port that functioned from the 6th until the early 3rd century BC, serving the needs of trade.

Fig. 8: Abdera: APAX survey: Loom weights (left) and grinding stones (right).

Storage Pithoi and Grinding Stones

Parts of large storage pithoi have been found in certain areas within the city, apparently for the storage of large quantities of agro-silvo-pastoral produce, which the fertile plain of the broader area of Abdera would offer.[28] Grinding stones have been recovered in considerable numbers dispersed in Abdera (fig. 8-right). They have been identified primarily within the habitation areas and most of them seem to have been part of the *oikos* tools. They are either triangular or ovoid in shape and appear to have been made from volcanic stone, some of which could have been coming (via the sea) from Nisyros in the southern Aegean, while others have a probable provenance from the Rhodopi Mountains and could have come through Nestos' River transportation or following that route. Furthermore, the recovery of some Olynthus-type mills (made of volcanic stones from Nisyros?) argues that in specific areas within the *polis* a larger scale flour production was taking place as well.[29]

Textiles

Clay loom weights have been found in considerable quantity scattered around the settlement (much like the grinding stones) thus suggesting that this was a common household activity which was important for the *oikos* economy and perhaps it was extended beyond it within the site (fig. 8-left) It also argues that there was locally enough available wool for making clothes, carpets, etc. Therefore it becomes clear that within the pastoral practices of this area, sheep was an important aspect, raised primarily for their wool. Linen may have also been locally produced and used in the looms in order to produce garments. The sandy clay soil is ideal for such a crop, which could be found close to the Nestos riverbeds.

Greeks and Thracians

In the northern part of the Xanthi plain, both the ancient text as well as the archaeological finds, suggest that the area was controlled for most part of the 1st millennium BC by the local Thracians.[30] Our ongoing survey has identified a few new sites, the largest of which share some common landscape features: They are located on slopes of prominent hills, in defensible positions, and they are extending to the lowland area around large streams. Moreover, the remains of slags strongly suggest the local working of metals as the historical sources have informed us. This also argues that they had a good contact and access to the metal sources situated in the mountainous part of Rhodopi. The rivers could have had a practical as well as a symbolic meaning to the Thracians for their everyday life as well as for the performance of rituals and cultic activities. Perhaps they had a different attitude towards streams and rivers in relation to the ones Greeks had.[31]

Conclusions

The local agro-silvo-pastoral produce and trade were the two basic pillars of the economy developed by the Greek colonists at Abdera. The access of metals through their contacts with the Thracians via inland and river routes was mutually beneficial for the two diverse cultural groups thus economy and trade played a central role in their interactions, relationship and prosperity. The sea remained the main route the Abderitans used to disseminate metals and other produce to the rest of the Aegean.

However, in the battle between the natural forces and human stubbornness, nature won. Nestos River gradually silted the port and led to the movement of the city at the late 4th and early 3rd century BC to the south ('South Enclosure') in search with a better harbour, causing the gradual abandonment of the 'North Enclosure'. The unhealthy climate continued to cause problems to the local population until the Hellenistic period. Lucian mentions an incident of the 3rd century BC when an epidemic struck the city with the main symptoms being severe 7-days fever and delirium. In this framework, it is very probable that the poor climate, the environmental conditions along with the moisture created the myth of *avdiritism* (i.e. folly) a quite bizarre conception since Abdera was also the homeland of the philosopher Democritus, the "father of modern atomic science".

Notes

[1] Cf. Hdt I 168–169; Strabo XIV 1,30 (C 644). Tiverios 2008, esp. 91–99, 104–107; recently Kallintzi 2017.

[2] Kallintzi 2011, passim; Kallintzi 2012.

[3] Koukouli-Chryssanthaki 2004; Kallintzi 2012, 132–136.

[4] Koukouli-Chryssanthaki 2004, 242–244; Motsiou 2016; Motsiou 2019.

[5] Koukouli-Chryssanthaki 2004, 244–246. This harbour was functioning between 525/520 BC and 490/480 BC; Kallintzi (forthcoming) connected the construction of the shipshed with the Persian fleet.

[6] Hdt. V 2, 2.

[7] Cf. Herodotos (VII 118–121) who mentions that Abdera was one of the strongest cities in Thrace; also, Pindar (Paean 2.60) praises its bountiful land.

[8] Syrides – Psilovikos 2004.

[9] Kallintzi 2021.

[10] Diodoros XIII 72, 1–2.

[11] Diodoros XIII 72, 2.

[12] Kallintzi 2012, 136–139.

[13] The project combines intensive surface survey, geomorphological studies and geophysical survey: Kallintzi et al. 2015, 2017, 2020.

[14] Kallintzi 2004; Kallintzi 2011, passim.

[15] Skarlatidou 2010.

[16] Agelarakis 2010.

[17] Kallintzi 2006; Kallintzi 2007; cf. Samiou 2004.

[18] Kallintzi 2007.

[19] Veligianni-Terzi 2004, 118 f. 122–125.

[20] Metal ores and slags are being studied by Dr. N. Nerantzis.

[21] May 1966; Chryssanthaki 2000; Chryssanthaki-Nagle 2007.

[22] Chryssanthaki-Nagle 2018.

[23] It is interesting to note that marble is, so far, absent in domestic architecture and only rarely found in relation to public buildings.

[24] They are being studied by Dr. D. Stoyanova.

[25] An overview in Cevizoğlou 2004. It is being studied by K. Chatziprokopiou and Dr. N. Dimakis.

[26] The pottery is being studied by Prof. E. Kefalidou, Dr. Ch. Kallini, Dr. J. Mourthos and Dr. P. Ilieva.

[27] They are being studied by Ch. Tzochev. For their secondary use as burial urns: Skarlatidou 2010, passim.

[28] For their secondary use as burial urns: Skarlatidou 2010, passim.

[29] Frankel 2003.

[30] Triantaphyllos 1990 & 1991.

[31] Triantaphyllos 2009.

Image Credits

Fig. 1–3: © Xanthi Ephorate of Antiquities. – Fig. 4: © Xanthi Ephorate of Antiquities; <hogsheadwine.files.wordpress.com/2012/06/03_thraceabdera tetradrachm411_386> (last access: 11th August 2019) [Tetradrachm]; <www.cointalk.com/threads/ancient-greek-abdera-thrace-tetrobol-247064> (last access: 11th August 2019) [Tetrobol with corn]. – Fig. 5–8: © Xanthi Ephorate of Antiquities.

References

Agelarakis 2010

A. P. Agelarakis, The Human Condition in the 7th Century BC in Abdera as Revealed through Physical and Forensic Anthropology, in: Skarlatidou 2010, 375–388.

Cevizoğlou 2004

H. Cevizoğlou, Archaic Relief Vases from Klazomenai, in: Moustaka et al. 2004, 185–198.

Chryssanthaki 2000

K. Chryssanthaki, L'histoire monétaire d'Abdère du VIe avant J.-C. au IIe siècle après J.-C. PhD thesis, Université Paris IV- Sorbonne, École Doctorale (Paris 2000).

Chryssanthaki-Nagle 2007

K. Chryssanthaki-Nagle, L'histoire monétaire d'Abdère en Thrace (VIe s. av. J.C.-IIe s. ap. J.-C.), Meletemata 51 (Athens 2007).

Chryssanthaki-Nagle 2018

K. Chryssanthaki-Nagle, "Εικονογραφία του νομισματοκοπείου των Αβδήρων. Εικόνα και νομισματική πολιτική", in: Obolos 13. Proceedings of the Seventh Scientific Meeting in Memory of Mando Oeconomides, Athens 20–21 April 2016 (Athens 2018) 59–69

Frankel 2003

R. Frankel, The Olynthus Mill. Its Origin, and Diffusion: Typology and Distribution, AJA 107, 2003, 1–21.

Kallintzi 2004

C. S. Kallintzi, Abdera. Organization and Utilisation of the Area Extra Muros, in: Moustaka et al. 2004, 271–289.

Kallintzi 2006

C. S. Kallintzi, Les nécropoles d'Abdère. Organisation de l'espace et rites funéraires, in: A.-M. Guimier-Sorbets – M. B. Hatzopoulos – Y. Morizot (eds.), Rois, cités, nécropoles: institutions, rites et monuments en Macédoine, Actes des colloques de Nanterre (Décembre 2002) et d'Athènes (Janvier 2004), Meletemata 45 (Athens 2006) 143–153.

Kallintzi 2007

C. S. Kallintzi, Κοσμήματα από το νεκροταφείο των αρχαίων Αβδήρων, in: Thrace in the Graeco-Roman World, Proceedings of the 10th International Congress of Thracology, Komotini-Alexandroupolis 18–23/10/2005 (Athens 2007) 255–272.

Kallintzi 2011

C. S. Kallintzi, Η χώρα των Αβδήρων. Συμβολή στην αρχαιολογία και ιστορική τοπογραφία του νότιου τμήματος του Νομού Ξάνθης. PhD thesis, University of Thessaly (Volos 2011), <http://thesis.ekt.gr/thesisBookReader/id/31737#page/1/ mode/2up>, <http://hdl.handle.net/10442/hedi/31737> (last access: 11th August 2021).

Kallintzi 2012

C. S. Kallintzi, Επίθεση και άμυνα στην πόλη των Αβδήρων, in: P. Adam-Veleni – K. Tzanavari (eds.), Δινήεσσα. Τιμητικός τόμος για την Κατερίνα Ρωμιοπούλου (Thessaloniki 2012) 131–140.

Kallintzi 2017

C.S. Kallintzi, Άβδηρα, in: A. Vlachopoulos – D. Tsiafaki 2017, Αρχαιολογία. Μακεδονία Θράκη (Athens 2017) 498–501.

Kallintzi 2021

C. S. Kallintzi, Οργάνωση της λατομικής δραστηριότητας και χρήσεις του λίθου στη χώρα και το άστυ των Αβδήρων, in: Z. I. Bonias – J. Y. Perreault (eds.), Άργιλος, 25 χρόνια έρευνας. Οργάνωση πόλης και χώρας στις αποικίες του βορείου Αιγαίου, 8ος – 3ος αι. π.Χ., 25–27/5/2017 (Athens 2021) 563–590.

Kallintzi forthcoming

C. S. Kallintzi, Abdera: The Sea Matters. Did the City Make Its Harbours, or Did the Harbours Make Their City?, in: International Workshop MARE THRACIUM, 3–4/11/2016, Römisch-Germanisches Zentralmuseum, Mainz, Germany (forthcoming).

Kallintzi et al. 2015

C. S. Kallintzi – M. Georgiadis – E. Kefalidou – I. Xydopoulos – M. Chrysaphi –K. Chatziprokopiou – D. Skoulariki – H. Orengo – A. Garcia, Αρχαιολογικό Πρόγραμμα Αβδήρων και Ξάνθης (ΑΠΑΞ): πρώτο έτος της επιφανειακής έρευνας, AErgoMak 29, 2015, 529–539.

Kallintzi et al. 2017

C. S. Kallintzi – M. Georgiadis – E. Kefalidou – M. Chrysaphi – K. Chatziprokopiou – D. Skoulariki – A. Garcia, Αρχαιολογικό Πρόγραμμα Αβδήρων και Ξάνθης (ΑΠΑΞ): τα αποτελέσματα των ετών 2016 και 2017, AErgoMak 31, 2017.

Kallintzi et al. 2020

C. S. Kallintzi – M. Georgiadis – E. Kefalidou – I. Xydopoulos, Greeks and Thracians at Abdera and the Xanthi Nestos Area in Aegean Thrace, in: J. Driessen – A. Vanzetti (eds.), Communication Uneven: Acceptance of and Resistance to Foreign Influences in the Connected Ancient Mediterranean – Aegis 20 (Louvain 2020) 129–146.

Koukouli-Chryssanthaki 2004

Ch. Koukouli-Chryssanthaki, The Archaic City of Abdera, in: Moustaka et al. 2004, 235–248.

May 1966

J. M. F. May, The Coinage of Abdera, 540–345 BC (London 1966).

Motsiou 2016

P. Motsiou, Μικρογραφικές υδρίες από το ιερό της Δήμητρας Αβδήρων – MA Thesis, National and Kapodistrian University of Athens, Dpt. of History and Archaeology (Athens 2016), <https://pergamos.lib.uoa.gr/uoa/dl/object/1327921> (last access: 11th August 2019)

Motsiou 2019
P. Motsiou, Υδρίσκες από το ιερό της Δήμητρας στα Άβδηρα: παρατηρήσεις για την κατασκευή και τη χρήση μικρογραφικών αγγείων σε ιερά του βόρειου Αιγαίου, in: E. Manakidou – A. Avramidou (eds.), Classical Pottery of the Northern Aegean and its Periphery, 480–323/300 BC – International Archaeological Conference, Thessaloniki 17–20/5/2017 (Thessaloniki 2019) 591–603.

Moustaka et al. 2004
A. Moustaka – E. Skarlatidou – M. C. Tzannes – Y. Ersoy (eds.), Klazomenai, Teos and Abdera: Metropoleis and Colony, International Symposium, Abdera, 20–21/10/2001 (Thessaloniki 2004).

Samiou 2004
Chr. Samiou, Hellenistic Graves at Abdera, in: Moustaka et al. 2004, 291–303.

Skarlatidou 2010
E. K. Skarlatidou, Το αρχαϊκό νεκροταφείο των Αβδήρων (Thessaloniki 2010).

Syrides – Psilovikos 2004
G. E. Syrides – A. A. Psilovikos, Geoarchaeological Investigations in the Area of Ancient Abdera, in: Moustaka et al. 2004, 351–459.

Tiverios 2008
M. Tiverios, Greek Colonization of the Northern Aegean, in: G. R. Tsetskhladze (ed.), Greek Colonisation. An Account of Greek Colonies and Other Settlements Overseas 2 (Leiden 2008) 1–154.

Triantaphyllos 1990
D. Triantaphyllos, Οχυρωματικοί Περίβολοι στην Ενδοχώρα της Αιγαιακής Θράκης, in: Ch. Koukouli-Chryssanthaki – O. Picard (eds.), Μνήμη Δ. Λαζαρίδη. Πόλις και Χώρα στην αρχαία Μακεδονία και Θράκη, Πρακτικά Αρχαιολογικού Συνεδρίου, Kavala, 9–11/5/1986 (Thessaloniki 1990) 683–699.

Triantaphyllos 1991
D. Triantaphyllos, Η Θράκη του Αιγαίου πριν από τον ελληνικό αποικισμό, Θρακική Επετηρίδα 7, 1991, 297–322.

Triantaphyllos 2009
D. Triantaphyllos, Η Θράκη από το Νέστο ως τον Έβρο πριν και μετά τον ελληνικό αποικισμό, in: Z. I. Bonias – J. Y. Perreault (eds.), Greeks and Thracians in Coastal and Inland Thrace during the Years before and after the Great Colonization, Proceedings of the International Symposium, Thasos, 26–27 September 2008 (Thasos 2009) 187–204.

Veligianni-Terzi 2004
Chr. Veligianni-Terzi, Οι Ελληνίδες πόλεις και το Βασίλειο των Οδρυσών, από Αβδήρων πόλεως μέχρι Ίστρου ποταμού (Thessaloniki 2004).

The Classical City on the Molyvoti Peninsula (Aegean Thrace): Landscape, Urban Development, and Economic Networks

Nathan T. Arrington – Domna Terzopoulou – Marina Tasaklaki – Eli Weaverdyck

The Rhodopi mountain range and its large, fertile plain dominate Aegean Thrace, a well-watered region with a few lakes and several lagoons. Between the Strymon and Evros Rivers, *emporia* and colonies were established during the Archaic period. From Paros, colonists founded Thasos, and later the Thasians established colonies on the Thracian coast, forming the so-called Thasian Peraia. Greeks from Asia Minor founded Abdera and colonists from Chios founded Maroneia at the foot of Mount Ismaros. Further to the east, the inhabitants of Samothrace (Aeolians and Ionians who had arrived there in the early 7th century BC) were active in foundations on the mainland (the Samothracian Peraia). Ainos, the easternmost colony of the Aegean Thracian coast, was established by Aeolians at the mouth of the Evros River.[1]

This paper discusses the walled city on the Molyvoti Peninsula in its river environment (fig. 1). The settlement was one of the four principal Greek establishments between the Nestos River and Mount Ismaros, and it flourished during the Classical period and was re-occupied during the Late Roman Period. We will focus here, firstly, on how rivers contributed to a dynamic and changing landscape and, secondly, how rivers configured regional trade networks.

Herodotus provides important information on the topography of Aegean Thrace when he describes the route of Xerxes' army from Asia to mainland Greece (Hdt. 7.108–109). The passages, and especially those that mention Maroneia and Stryme, have been subject to considerable discussion and have led to varying reconstructions of the regional topography. During the 1950s, professor George Bakalakis combined the report of Herodotus with the excavation record, and suggested that the walled ancient city on the Molyvoti Peninsula should be identified with Stryme, the only Thasian colony founded in the 7th century BC to the east of the Nestos River, and a site known from other literary sources as both a polis and an emporion.[2] His view was widely accepted, but some scholars continue to express reservations about the identification.[3] Without epigraphic testimony, the debate will probably continue, and this is not the place to lay out the evidence in support of the identification. We may, however, point out that most of the arguments against seeing the city as Ancient Stryme stem from assumptions about the size and nature of an emporion, yet a consideration of other factors of the archaeological record, including the settlement's relationship to the landscape and rivers, shows how it was a "place between" land and sea well-situated for trade, commerce, and interaction of a type associated with emporia.

Fig. 1: The settlement on the Molyvoti Peninsula identified as Ancient Stryme.

The evidence discussed here stems from a new period of research for the city on the Molyvoti Peninsula that began in 2013.[4] The Molyvoti, Thrace, Archaeological Project (MTAP) aims to study the settlement on the peninsula, hereafter called Stryme, in its regional context. The five-year expedition is a cooperation between the Ephorate of Antiquities of Rhodopi (Komotini) and the American School of Classical Studies at Athens, represented by Princeton University. The project combines geomorphological studies, geophysical survey, and surface survey with focused excavation. The Molyvoti Peninsula is located southwest of modern Komotini, at the end of a long plain. Today, widespread cultivation takes place between the Rhodopi mountains and the Aegean Sea, predominantly of cotton and wheat. In the area of the ancient site there is one large lake, Lake Mitrikon, and two rivers, the Vosvozis River and the Filiouris River. Lake Mitrikon is usually identified as ancient Lake Ismaris, and the Filiouris River as the Lissos River (Hdt. 7.108–109). During the 4th century BC the city occupied an area of approximately 60 hectares and had probably two harbors. On the west side of the city, a lagoon existed also during the habitation period of the city.

The plain that extends to the north of the fortified settlement as far as Lake Ismaris, is the area known as Mitrikon. In this extended landscape there are more than 30 tumuli. The tumuli are scattered across an area roughly 5 km long and 3 km wide, starting 500 m north of the city wall and ending near Lake Mitrikon. Most follow a linear path along the eastern ridge of the hinterland, almost certainly indicating the presence of an important

Fig. 2: Satellite image of the Molyvoti Peninsula and its hinterland.

road running north from the city. The identification of a possible Ionic temple near Lake Mitrikon further supports this hypothesis. The locations of other tumuli cannot be explained with reference to this road: there are eight tumuli on the western ridge and three near a stream delta that fall outside the linear pattern. These might have been located on secondary roads or they could represent burials on private estates.

Today the mouth of the Filiouris River is located ca. 3.5 km from the wall of the city, and Lake Mitrikon is ca. 4.5 km distant. This was not always the case. The satellite image shows quite clearly how the area around the river, which is not cultivated, is a coastal marsh-swamp, suggesting how alluviation and river deposits may have changed the location of bodies of water and even of the coastline itself (fig. 2). During our project, a team from the University of Aristotle at Thessaloniki, led by George Syrides and Konstantinos Vouvalidis, explored the geomorphology of the coast and the area around the lake. A core adjacent to the lake provided valuable information. In the following discussion, we draw on their forthcoming report as well as other published studies.[5] The core revealed a stratum from ca. 3500–1500 BC with marine deposits and microfaunal evidence for marine species characteristic of shallow marine environments. In addition, there were some fresh water indicators, probably transported into the area by a stream. The next stratum, from ca. 1500–1000 BC, continued to represent a marine deposit, but there were more fresh water indicators, probably indicating something like a lagoon that still communicated with the sea. In a subsequent stratum, associated with the period of the city's foundation, from ca. 1000 BC to the turn of the millennium, evidence showed that there was a closed lagoon, and by the turn of the millennium, a fresh water environment (Lake Mitrikon) with river activity (the Vosvozis River) had formed.

In short, what this geomorphological data indicates is that the sea once extended as far as the location of the present day lake. Unfortunately, the strata in the core are not so precise as to date the formation of the lake closely. What we know, however, is that in the Archaic period, at the time of the foundation of Stryme, there was a lagoon and river activity in the area of the present-day lake, and that the lake formed sometime between 1000 BC and the turn of the millennium. As the only fresh water lake in Thrace, it is almost certainly Lake Ismaris, which Herodotus mentions when he describes the route of Xerxes in the 5th century BC, although its exact placement and size probably shifted somewhat over time. Currently it is 3 km^2 in size, with an average depth of 1 m.

The important point is that the coastline was a dynamic environment, and that geographic contours around the city changed quite quickly. As the two rivers brought sediments into the lake and delta, the coastline extended out towards the Molyvoti Peninsula. Only in recent times did this situation become more stable. Specifically, in the 1970s, a channel was cut for the Vosvozis River, changing its entry point to the northwest of the lake, so that sediment was deposited in the lake itself, and a second channel was cut through the delta plain to connect the lake with the sea.

The pollen from the core next to the lake provides evidence on how humans engaged with this dynamic landscape. The stratum from ca. 3500–1500 BC revealed the presence of a rich deciduous forest. Mountainous forests were also detected, with conifers and beech trees. Human presence in the area could be traced by the occurrence of several apophytes and coprophilous fungi, but there was no evidence of cereal cultivation. From ca. 1500–1000 BC, the landscape became more open as the mountainous forests retreated, although Mediterranean forests with evergreen oak, pine, and juniper remained part of the landscape. The increase of ruderal herb vegetation, the high diversity of apophyte taxa, and the presence of coprophilous fungal spores indicate human presence and the implementation of grazing activities, while charcoal shows that there were some significant regional fires. This activity probably should be associated with regional Thracians who were predominantly pastoral and occupied the land prior to Greek colonization. In fact, when the course of the Filiouri River was moved in 1973, Diamantis Triantaphyllos was able to excavate a Thracian cemetery at Ampelia, 3 km SE of Mikro Doukato.[6]

Unfortunately, we do not have much data from the core for pollen related to the period when Stryme itself was occupied, and our next evidence comes from the turn of the millennium. At this time, the retreat of the forest was more pronounced, and oak and deciduous trees were scarce. But there is not much evidence for human vegetation and cultivation in the area in the pollen record. This correlates with the abandonment of Stryme in the 3rd century BC. Although our surface survey has shown that activity did continue in the chora, evidently there was little cultivation, and rural activity was minimal.

As forests retreated and agriculture took hold, the geomorphological processes described above (i.e., alluviation and silting) created marshy conditions in the region of Stryme. The health hazards of such an environment tend to be emphasized, and certainly from nearby Abdera there are many ancient sources linking the swampy environment with illness and disease. Yet wetlands also support abundant and variegated animal and plant life, and they offered a rich range of resources for the community at Stryme.[7] Today, no fewer than 233 types of birds in the region of the Ismaris Lake have been recorded. We can imagine a similar faunal variety in antiquity, and bones from the archaeological site indicate extensive engagement with this diverse landscape. Zooarchaeologist Demetrios Brellas has identified bones from a wide variety of animals that once flourished in the wetlands. These include geese, swans, cranes, storks, coots, flamingo, cormorants, as well as several varieties of duck. Additionally, species of fish, such as mullet and shad, which thrive in the brackish waters of Stryme's coastal wetlands today, have also been identified.

The fresh water of the lake and rivers were also an important source of fish. Bones from catfish, freshwater salmonids, and particularly those of various species of cyprinids are common at the site. In addition to faunal evidence for the importance of fish and fishing at the site, fishing implements, such as bronze fish hooks and lead fish weights, contribute to the picture. It is difficult to date these objects by morphology or style, but they come from both the Classical and Late Roman levels. Some of these tools, of course, may have been used in the sea as well as the lakes and rivers, but the bones indicate that people engaged just as much if not more with their fresh water as their salt water environments.

The wetlands also provided an excellent place to pasture animals. The faunal assemblage from the site indicates a strong preponderance of sheep, which would thrive in this type of landscape. In the Ottoman period, maps and other historical documents show that herders would come from the mountains to the marshy plains in the winter to graze their animals.[8] Still today, the area around the lake and the river delta is frequented by grazing sheep.

While the marshes offered unique opportunities and resources to the community, they also presented constraints. In particular, the wetland environment could create health hazards, and residents of Stryme may have suffered from similar maladies as the people of Abdera. At Stryme, we lack the type of literary record that could document such travails, and we may only hypothesize that environmental factors contributed to the decline of the city in the Classical-Hellenistic period. Activity at the site petered out in the 3rd century BC, with no destruction horizon. There are, of course, many possible reasons for the termination of settlement, including the deterioration of regional security and trade networks, but one factor was the changing environmental conditions, as alluviation and silting intensified the marsh nature of the landscape.

Rivers, therefore, contributed to the formation of a landscape at once dynamic, fertile, and hazardous in which coastlines shifted relatively rapidly, a lake took shape, and wetland conditions emerged. In addition, the two rivers played a role in the development of trade networks. Both served as important routes of communication, linking the maritime site with inland resources and communities. River trade in ancient Greece and the Balkans is usually not considered significant, but this view may need to be reassessed. Three big rivers that arise in central Thrace and flow into the Aegean Sea certainly were navigable: the Strymon, Nestos and Evros Rivers, the latter a liquid highway until the beginning of the 20th century.[9] The importance of rivers for Classical emporia has been clearly demonstrated by the site of Bulgarian Pistiros, and Zosia Archibald has repeatedly drawn attention to the interconnections between coastal sites and the hinterland.[10] Might minor rivers have played an important role, too? River transport was less costly than land transport, and in antiquity, as today, land, sea and river transport complemented each other.[11]

The Vosvozis and Filiouris Rivers are not particularly deep today, but they may have been more substantial in antiquity. We have seen that the changes in the geomorphology of the area are significant enough that we should not assume on the basis of current appearances that rivers were not navigable in antiquity. Moreover, recent records show that from 1966 to 1999, rainfall averaged 507 mm, with a range from 270 to 876 mm, and a long drought from 1981 to 1993. Assuming that a similar degree of variability existed in antiquity as well, it is possible that at least in some years the rivers were navigable by rafts or canoes. A shallow boat found near the village of Peschcannoe (Ukraine) carrying 15 Greek gold-plated vessels is the type of transport vessel one can imagine on rivers that were not particularly deep and that was engaged in trans-cultural communication (fig. 3).[12]

The Vosvozis and Filiouris Rivers provided different degrees of connectivity with the hinterland. The Vosvozis River flows from the mountains of Thrace. The location of the river near the site and the discovery in our campaign of a few Thracian coins, inscriptions, and sherds suggest some type of connection between the emporion and Thracians.[13] Although the mountain range of Rhodopi appears to be an insurmountable barrier to communication, in the 16th century, Komotini's (Ott. Gümülcine) administrative zone (*sancak*) included towns in present-day Buglaria.[14] In other words, in at least one pre-modern period, the two sides of the mountains were closely entwined. The Makaza Pass, now a highway and border crossing, offers an important point of connection. Further west, the ancient site of Linos, in the foothills of the mountains, has an archaeological record that closely matches Stryme in terms of chronology and artifact type, and it may have been part of a broader network of communication across the mountains.[15] The Vosvozis River running across the plain

Fig. 3: The Peshchannoe canoe in the National Museum of the History of Ukraine, Kiev with Philip Katz and Christopher Parmenter for scale. Some of the Greek bronze vessels found with the canoe appear in the display case in the back left.

could participate in this network, helping to transport goods on their final journey down from the mountains and through the plain.

The Filiouris River offered a different path for connectivity. Bending toward the northeast, the river, almost certainly to be equated with the ancient Lissos River (there is no other river in the vicinity that could meet Herodotus' description), connected Stryme to the fertile valley behind the hills of Maroneia. The archaeological record at Stryme supports a close relationship between Maroneia and Stryme, which the river would have facilitated. Like other emporia, Stryme, which did not mint its own coins and was not on the Athenian Tribute lists, was politically and economically dependent on a regional power. The abundance of Maronitan coins from Stryme and the presence of even a few weights testify to its close connection to Maroneia, itself a settlement known for its strong ties to Thracians, including to the Odrysian court across the mountain pass.[16]

A consideration of both of these rivers re-orients our view of the seaside trading port, drawing attention to its landward connections. Indeed, surface survey of Stryme's chora has shown a much more extensive engagement with the landscape than the term emporion might suggest, which generally implies a static node

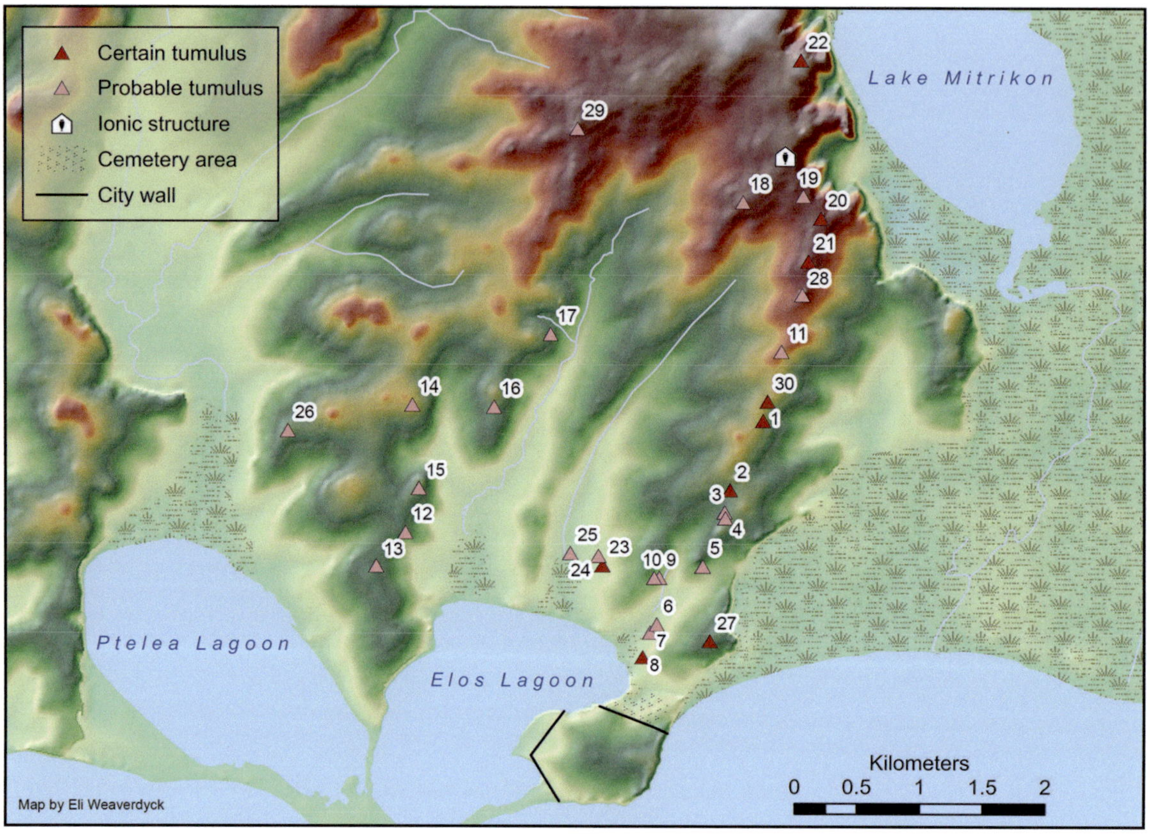

Fig. 4: The tumuli and Ionic temple in the *chora* of Stryme. The tumuli document the purported path of a road leading toward the mountains.

oriented toward the sea. In addition to abundant surface sherds that testify to a busy landscape dotted with farms, there are more than 30 tumuli across an area roughly 5 km long and 3 km wide (fig. 4). The majority almost certainly follow the course of an ancient road that connected the settlement with the mountains. The identification of an Ionic temple near Lake Mitrikon supports this hypothesis. Outside the linear pattern, there are eight tumuli on the western ridge and three near a stream delta, which might have been located on secondary roads or could represent burials on private estates.

In conclusion, although seaside trading points are usually interpreted in terms of their connection to the sea, this paper has demonstrated the importance of rivers for understanding the relationship of emporia to dynamic environmental conditions and for revealing how they participated in mainland trade networks. Located on the Thracian Sea, Stryme maintained a close connection with a fertile chora and a rich wetland created and enabled by fluvial activity. Rivers also linked the settlement to powerful Maroneia and to resources across the plain and even mountains. No doubt the rivers in part explain the puzzling choice of the Molyvoti Peninsula for settlement. Unlike most other colonies in Aegean Thrace, Stryme was not located close to sources of valuable metals, instead occupying an important geo-political place in a fertile and changing landscape nourished and traversed by rivers.

Notes

[1] On colonization in Thrace, see esp. Tiverios 2008. On the history of the individual settlements, Loukopoulou 2004 offers an excellent starting point.

[2] Bakalakis 1958, 91–97; Bakalakis 1967.

[3] Esp. Loukopoulou – Psoma 2008.

[4] Arrington et al. 2013–2017; Arrington et al. 2016. On the work of the 1990s, see Triantaphyllos – Terzopoulou 2012, with further bibliography.

[5] Pisinarasa et al. 2007; Katsavouni et al. 2012; Karadimou et al. 2016. The geomorphological and palynological studies of MTAP will be presented in more detail in the project's final publication, which is currently in preparation.

[6] Triantaphyllos 1983.

[7] On wetlands, see Horden – Purcell 2000, 186–190.

[8] The Ottoman records will be presented by Emily Neumeier and Sotirios Dimitriadis in the project's final publication.

[9] De Boer 2010.

[10] Most recently, Archibald 2016.

[11] On cost, see Duncan-Jones 1982, 368.

[12] Tsetskhladze 1998, 65.

[13] For Thracian coins found in the past in Molyvoti see: Gatzolis et al. 2007.

[14] Sarinay 2003, 138. We owe this information to the research of Emily Neumeier and Sotirios Dimitriadis, who will present their findings in detail in the project's final publication.

[15] Anagnostopoulou-Chatzipolychroni 1991.

[16] Psoma et al. 2008.

Image Credits

Fig. 1: Map by Eli Weaverdyck. – Fig. 2: by the authors. – Fig. 3: Photo by Samuel Holzman. – Fig. 4: Map by Eli Weaverdyck.

References

Archibald 2016

Z. H. Archibald, Moving Upcountry: Ancient Travel from Coastal Ports to Inland Harbours, in: K. Höghammar – B. Alroth – A. Lindhagen (eds.), Ancient Ports: The Geography of Connections. Proceedings of an International Conference at the Department of Archaeology and Ancient History, Uppsala University, 23–25 September 2010 (Uppsala 2016) 37–64.

Anagnostopoulou-Chatzipolychroni 1991

E. Anagnostopoulou-Chatzipolychroni, Ανασκαφικές έρευνες στο Ληνό Ν. Ροδόπης, AErgoMak 5, 1991, 477–487.

Arrington et al. 2013–2017

N. T. Arrington – D. Terzopoulou – M. Tasaklaki, Μολυβωτή – Αρχαιολογικό Πρόγραμμα Θράκης: 'Αρχαία Στρύμη', ADelt 68, 2013–2017, 751–755.

Arrington et al. 2016

N. T. Arrington – D. Terzopoulou – M. Tasaklaki – M. Lawall – D. Brellas – C. White, The Molyvoti, Thrace, Archaeological Project: 2013 Preliminary Report, Hesperia 85, 2016, 1¬–64.

Bakalakis 1958

G. Bakalakis, Προανασκαφικές έρευνες στη Θράκη (Thessaloniki 1958).

Bakalakis 1967

G. Bakalakis, Ανασκαφὴ Στρύμης (Thessaloniki 1967).

De Boer 2010

J. G. De Boer, River Trade in Eastern and Central Thrace from the Bronze Age till the Hellenistic Period, Eirene 46, 2010, 176–189.

Duncan-Jones 1982

R. Duncan-Jones, The Economy of the Roman Empire: Quantitative Studies (Cambridge 1982).

Gatzolis et al. 2007

Chr. Gatzolis – V. Poulios – D. Terzopoulou, Coins of the Thracian Kings and Rulers from Western Thrace, Eastern and Central Macedonia (5th–3rd century BC), in: A. Iakovidou (ed.), Proceedings of the 10th International Congress of Thracology (Athens 2007) 176– 187.

Horden – Purcell 2000

P. Horden – N. Purcell, The Corrupting Sea: A Study of Mediterranean History (Oxford 2000).

Karadimou et al. 2016

G. Karadimou – K. Vouvalidis – G. Syrides – O. Koukousioura – E. Aidona, Geomorphological and Paleoenvironmental Changes of Ismarida Lake during Holocene (N. Greece), Bulletin of the Geological Society of Greece 50, 2016, 424–433.

Katsavouni et al. 2012

S. Katsavouni – D. Papadimos – Ch. Doulgeris, Αναγνώριση των μεταβολών στις χρήσεις γης, στις γειτνιάζουσες με τη λίμνη Ισμαρίδα εκτάσεις, in: The Goulandris Natural History Museum – Greek Biotope/Wetland Centre (Thermi 2012) <http://repository.biodiversity-info.gr/bitstream/11340/975/1/863.pdf> (last access: 11th August 2019)

Loukopoulou 2004
L. D. Loukopoulou, Thrace from Nestos to Hebros, in: M. H. Hansen – T. H. Nielsen (eds.), An Inventory of Archaic and Classical 'Poleis' (Oxford 2004) 870–884.
Loukopoulou – Psoma 2008
L. D. Loukopoulou – S. E. Psoma, Maroneia and Stryme Revisited: Some Problems of Historical Topography, in: L. D. Loukopoulou – S. E. Psoma (eds.), Thrakika Zetemata 1, Meletemata 58 (Athens 2008) 55–86.
Pisinarasa et al. 2007
V. Pisinarasa – C. Petalasa – V. A. Tsihrintzisa – E. Zaganab, A Groundwater Flow Model for Water Resources Management in the Ismarida Plain, North Greece, Environmental Modeling and Assessment 12, 2007, 75–89.
Psoma et al. 2008
S. Psoma – Ch. Karadima – D. Terzopoulou, The Coins from Maroneia and the Classical City at Molyvoti: A Contribution to the History of Aegean Thrace, Meletēmata 62 (Athens 2008).
Sarinay 2003
Y. Sarinay (ed.), 167 Numarali Muhâsebe-i Vilâyet-i Rûm-ili defteri: 937/1530 (Istanbul 2003).
Tiverios 2008
M. Tiverios, Greek Colonization of the Northern Aegean, in: G. R. Tsetskhladze (ed.), Greek Colonisation. An Account of Greek Colonies and Other Settlements Overseas 2 (Leiden 2008) 1–154.
Triantaphyllos 1983
D. Triantaphyllos, Αρχαϊκό νεκροταφείο στη Δυτική Θράκη, ASAtene 61, 1983, 174–207.
Triantaphyllos – Terzopoulou 2012
D. Triantaphyllos – D. Terzopoulou, Ανασκαφή Στρύμης(;), in: P. Adam-Veleni – K. Tzanavari (eds.), Δινήεσσα: Τιμητικός τόμος για την Κατερίνα Ρωμιοπούλου (Thessaloniki 2012) 140–156.
Tsetskhladze 1998
G. R. Tsetskhladze, Greek Colonisation in the Black Sea Area: Stages, Models, and Native Population, in: G. R. Tsetskhladze (ed.), The Greek Colonisation of the Black Sea Area: Historical Interpretation of Archaeology (Stuttgart 1998) 9–68.

Doriskos. "Αἰγιαλός καὶ πεδίον μέγα". A Harbour on the West Side of the Evros River

Chryssa Karadima

Doriskos is reported by the ancient writer ps.Scylax (Periplous 67) as a "defensive wall" (*τεῖχος*) and by Herodotos (7.58-59) as a "seashore" and as "a plain of great extent" in Thrace, but also as an important fortified post (royal wall – *τεῖχος βασιλήιον*) of the Persians, where a permanent garrison was installed following Darius I's campaign against the Scythians in 514 BC. In 480 BC Xerxes, marching from the gulf of Melas first reached Ainos, an Aiolian colony, then passed by Lake Stentoris and finally arrived to Doriskos, i.e. the large plain around the delta, on the west side of the Evros River. The area served as a convenient place for reviewing and mustering the army of Xerxes' and as a supply center where he had laid up stores of provision. It had great strategic importance being located on the overland corridor that connects Asia with Europe and the Aegean coast with the Thracian hinterland through the Evros River, which was navigable.

Fig. 1: The acropolis of Doriskos: Part of the excavated area, 2007.

Fig. 2: Clay mould for arrow heads, surface find from Doriskos.

Grigorios Euthymiou and Georgios Bakalakis already by 1955 and 1960, respectively, had come to understand the significance of the site on "Sarayia" Hill, east of the modern village of Doriskos and south of Feres, which was identified as the ancient Doriskos. Small-scale excavations conducted by Diamantis Triantafyllos in 1971 have revealed sections of the fortification wall of the 4th century BC, a paved road and some looted tombs. Since 1991 systematic surface collections conducted on the site have yielded many finds which date from the Prehistoric through the late Hellenistic times.

The former 19th Ephorate of Prehistoric and Classical Antiquities (now Ephorates of Xanthi, Rhodopi and Evros) in conjunction with the Geophysics Division of the Department of Geology at the Aristotle University of Thessaloniki (in collaboration

Fig. 3: Bronze coin of Doriskos.

Fig. 4: Stamped amphora handle of Samothrace found in Doriskos.

with Prof. Grigorios Tsokas) has carried out two consecutive seasons of geophysical survey (2005–2006) on the site of Doriskos (fig. 5). These surveys have provided clear indications for the existence of ancient residential remains. Magnetic and resistance mapping were used to investigate an area of around 14.400 m^2. In particular, the resistance anomalies show clear rectangular shapes that appeared closed in most cases. Also, long linear anomalies were detected.

An initial six-week excavation campaign in the fall of 2007 was followed by a second season in 2010, which revealed part of the fortification wall and of the urban plan of the Hellenistic city confirming the results of the geophysical surveys. The archaeological evidence provides the image of a small fortified settlement (figs. 1. 2) whose inhabitants made their living through cereal cultivation, textile production, fishing and trade, as attested by archaeological finds that specifically include grinding mills, wine presses, clay loom weights, coins of the Classical and Hellenistic periods (fig. 3), transport amphoras from Thasos, Akanthos, Ainos, Samothrace (fig. 4) and southeastern Aegean trade centers, as well as fine and common-ware pottery, coming mainly from neigbouring Ainos. The large number of amphora material, especially from the centers of Ainos and Samothrace, found in quantities whithin the site but also along the Evros River in the interior of Thrace (in sites like Kabyle, Seythopolis

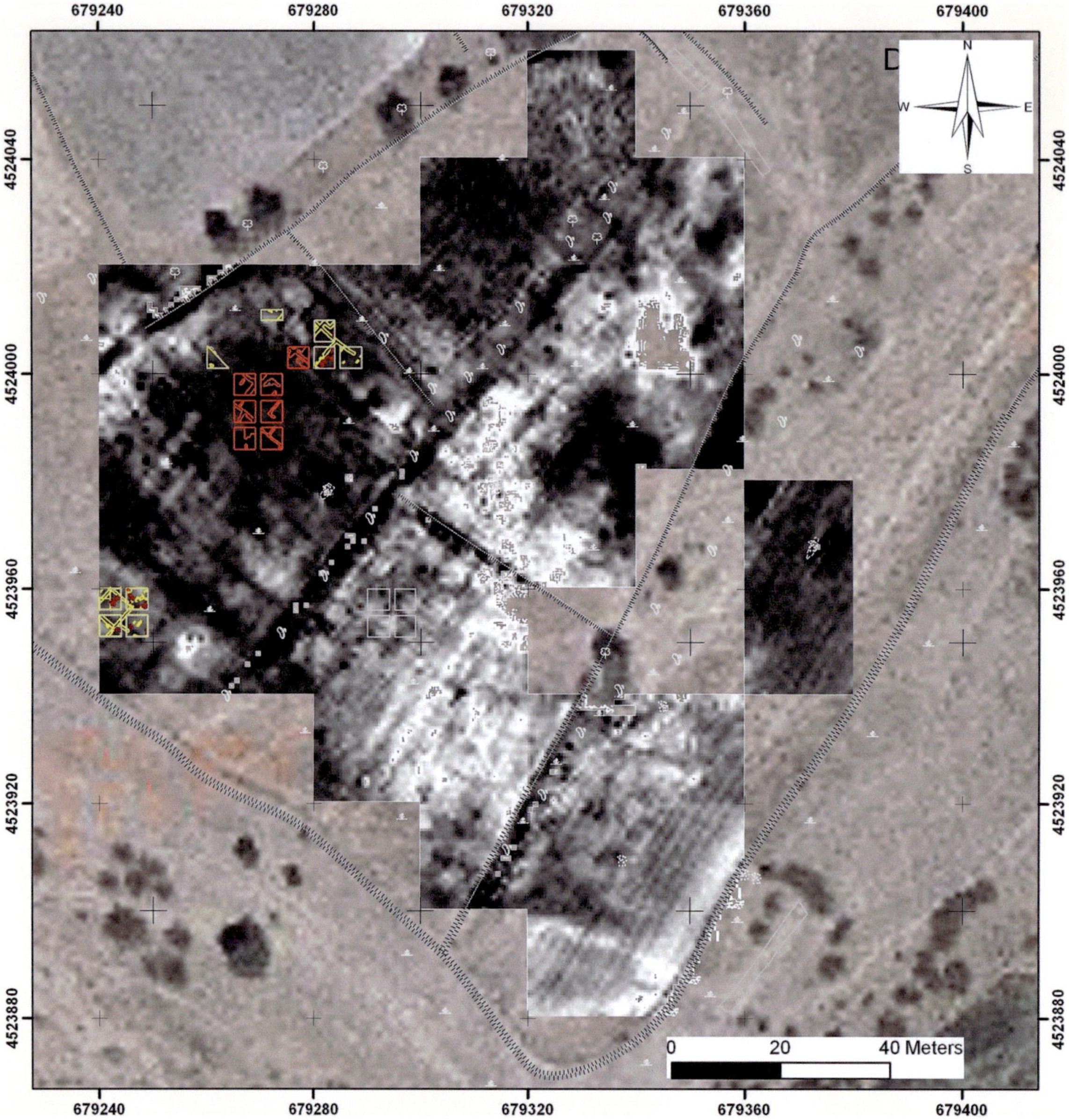

Fig. 5: The acropolis of Doriskos: Geophysical survey and excavated areas.

and Emporium Pistiros) testify to the navigable nature of the River Evros and the importance of Doriskos as a trade point.

In addition, the evidence of coins has highlighted the trade contacts that existed between the cities of Thrace and the Aegean Islands (Ainos, Maroneia, Zone, Madytos and Samothrace) as well as between the Macedonian and Thracian kings and dynasts (Philip II, Alexander III, Cassander, Lysimachos, Antiochos II and Sparadokos). The archaeological evidence supports also the hypothesis that Athens controlled Doriskos, at least before the Macedonian occupation by Philip II: The only coin type known so far from Doriskos' own mint has the head of Athena on the obverse, the name of the city (ΔΟΡΙ[ΣΚΟΣ]) and an owl on the reverse, and has been found during our excavations (fig. 3).

Image Credits

Fig. 1: © Rhodopi Ephorate of Antiquities. Photo: Ch. Karadima. – Fig. 2–4: © Rhodopi Ephorate of Antiquities. Photo: St. Stournaras. – Fig. 5: © Rhodopi Ephorate of Antiquities.

References

Bakalakis 1961
G. Bakalakis, Αρχαιολογικές έρευνες στη Θράκη 1959–60, Δημοσιεύματα της Θρακικής Εστίας Θεσσαλονίκης (Thessaloniki 1961).

Bakalakis 1963
G. Bakalakis, Αρχαιολογικαί Έρευναι εν Θράκη, ADelt 17, 1963, 258–261.

Bakalakis 1991
G. Bakalakis, Καταληπτήρας από τον Δορίσκο (Έβρου), in: Αρμός, Τιμητικός τόμος στον Ν. Κ. Μουτσόπουλο (Thessaloniki 1991) 1225–1229.

Euthymiou 1954
G. Euthymiou, Διάφορα όστρακα εκ Δορίσκου, Αρχείον του Λαογραφικού και Γλωσσικού Θησαυρού 19, 1954, 150–153.

Euthymiou 1955
G. Euthymiou, Μαρμάρινον αγαλμάτιον Αρτέμιδος εκ Δορίσκου, Αρχείον του Λαογραφικού και Γλωσσικού Θησαυρού 20, 1955, 134–138.

IThrAeg
L. D. Loukopoulou – M. G. Parissaki – S. Psoma – A. Zournatzi, Inscriptiones antiquae partis Thraciae quae ad ora maris Aegaei sita est (Praefecturae Xanthes, Rhodopes et Hebri). Ediderunt et commentariis sermone graeco conscriptis instruxerunt, Research Centre for Greek and Roman Antiquity, National Hellenic Research Foundation (Athens 2005) .

Karadima 2004
Ch. Karadima, Ainos, an Unknown Amphora Production Centre in the Evros Delta, in: J. Eiring – J. Lund (eds), Transport Amphorae and Trade in the Eastern Mediterranean, Acts of the International Colloquium at the Danish Institute at Athens, 26–29 September 2002, Danish Institute at Athens (Athens 2004)155–161.

Karadima forthcoming a
Ch. Karadima, Αρχαιολογικές έρευνες στον αρχαίο Δορίσκο. Τα πρώτα αποτελέσματα, AErgo Mak 30, 2016 (forthcoming).

Karadima forthcoming b
Ch. Karadima, Coastal Settlements of the Aegean Thrace between Evros River and Lake Vistonis, in: Archaeology and History of Coastal Landscapes and Islands of the Thracian Sea during Antiquity and Byzantine Empire, workshop organized by the Römisch-Germanisches Zentralmuseum Mainz, 3.–4.11.2016 (forthcoming).

Triantaphyllos 1975
D. Triantaphyllos, Δορίσκος, ADelt 26, 1975, 439–440.

Tsokas et al. 2007
G. Tsokas - G. Vargemezis - A. Stampolidis – Ch. Karadima, Γεωφυσική έρευνα στον αρχαίο Δορίσκο, AErgoMak 21, 2007, 471–476.

Ainos – A Hub between Sea and Inland

Thomas Schmidts

Ainos, today Enez, is located in the westernmost area of Turkish Thrace, in the direct vicinity to the Meriç/Evros (ancient Hebros) estuary, which is today the border between Turkey and Greece. Due to a siltation process, Enez is today 4 km distant of the shoreline. In Antiquity and in Byzantine times it had been a harbour city at a bay open to the sea.

History of Ainos

Ainos was founded as a Greek colony in the late 7th or 6th century BC and had been an important member of the Delian league in the 5th century BC. The production of wine and its export is proven by stamps on amphorae of the 5th and 4th centuries BC. For this period Ainos was considered to be amongst the wealthiest cities of the northern Aegean. In Hellenistic and Roman times, the importance of Ainos seems to have declined. The main argument for this was the reduction of the coin production. The city flourished again during Late Antiquity. In Byzantine times, Ainos was still a trade hub. Since 1265, the Venetians established a commercial settlement at Ainos and between 1384 and 1453 it was ruled by members of the Genoese Gattilusi family.

Monuments and Archaeological Research

Although archaeological research in Ainos started in the early 20th century and is continuously conducted by the Istanbul University since the 1980's, the development of the topography in ancient and Byzantine times are still unclear in many aspects. The best-known monument of Byzantine Ainos is a large 12th century AD church, situated inside the Byzantine castle (fig 1.5). Another church of remarkable dimensions called Kral Kizi Kilisesi is situated southeast of the city (fig. 1.17). The construction of the church can be dated in the period from the late 6th to the 9th century AD. Also, traces of a preceding church can be recognised.

Structures datable in Antiquity are less known. A Roman villa (fig. 1.9) and a well-built section of a street give at least an indication that in Roman times the city was not as poor as it was believed based on the study of local coinage. Two large ancient cemeteries, located respectively southeast and east of Enez, existed until the Late Antiquity. They were a major subject of the excavation activities of the Istanbul University team and yielded extraordinary grave furniture.

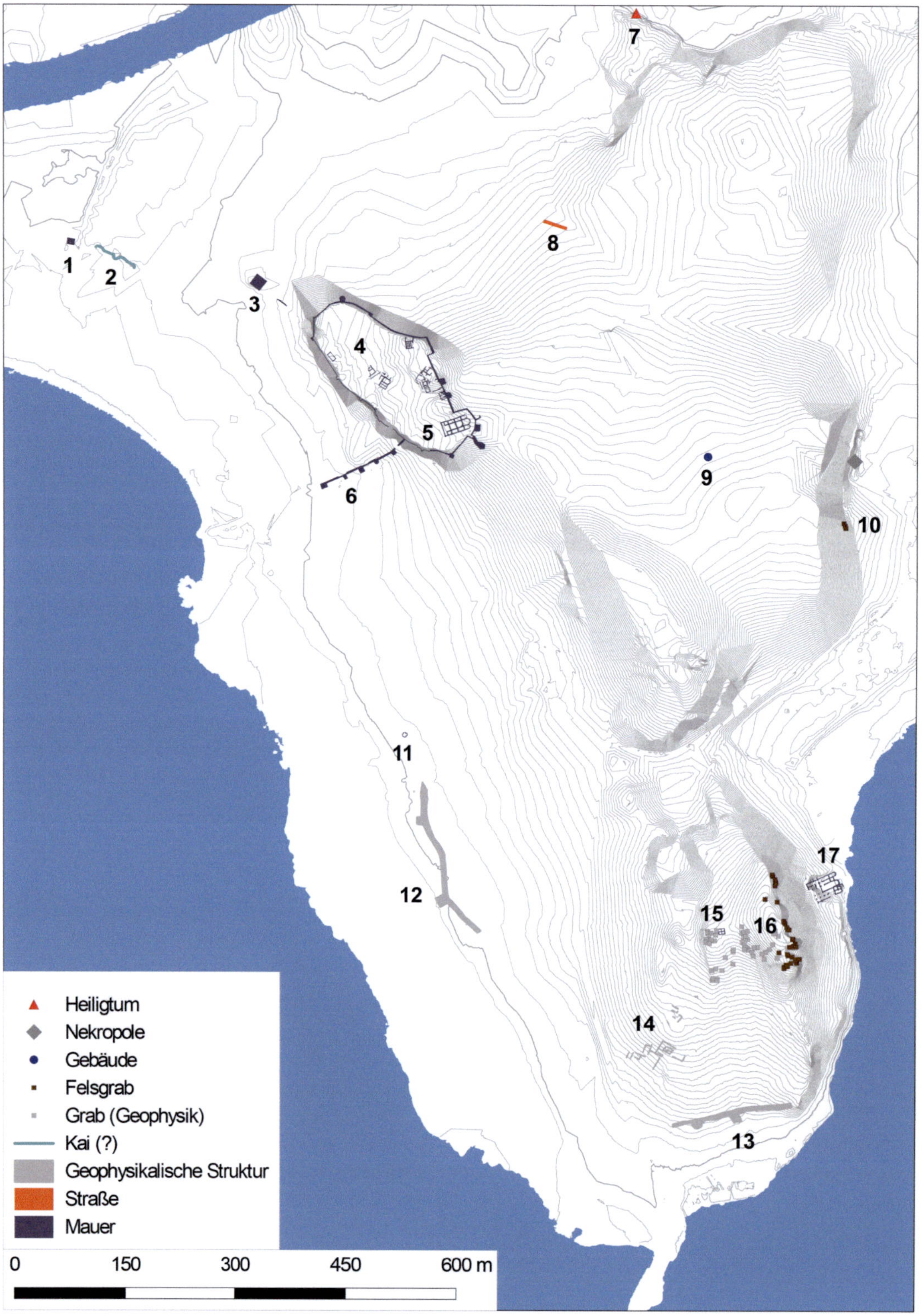

Fig. 1: Map of the remains in the urban area of Ainos-Enez.

The Ainos Project (2012–2018)

The multidisciplinary project entitled "The Thracian harbour city Ainos in Roman and Byzantine Times – Development of a Hub in a Changing Environment" is part of the Priority Program of German Research Foundation "Harbours from the Roman Period to the Middle Ages". It is conducted by the author together with Prof. Helmut Brückner (University of Cologne). During the field campaigns the littoral zones were investigated extensively by geophysical prospections and geoarchaeological drillings.

One of the major results was the detection of two sections of an unknown ancient city wall on the land tongue south of the modern city (fig. 1.12–13). The section in the west is following a zigzag line, which is a characteristic feature of Hellenistic city walls. It shows that the extension of the city was larger than estimated before and that it was built at a time of an assumed decline.

Byzantine fortifications near the lagoon, west and northwest of the Byzantine castle, had been interpreted as a part of a harbour. The main monument is a long wall of 130 m with 5 towers, which is orientated towards the lagoon (fig. 1.6). Future excavation may show that the wall had been erected with three towers in the middle Byzantine era, probably not before the 11th century AD. Two rectangular towers belong to a later period, which can be dated by an emblem of the Gattilusi family, Genoese ruler of Ainos from 1385 to 1453. Also the geoarchaeological research provides information on the development of this area. There has been no water between the walls in Byzantine times. A harbour could have been at the western front end of the wall where a low sedimentation rate between the 11th century BC and 14th century AD may indicate the dredging of a harbour area.

The major research focus of the project has been the harbour sites. Huge masonry in the water was described by Albert Dumont who visited Ainos in 1868, but the information is confusing. Potential harbour sites could be identified by the interpretation of geoarchaeological drilling cores in different areas around the ancient and Byzantine city. The survey and the documentary sources strengthen the impression of a large-scale use of the big lagoon and the possible existence of an outer harbour southwest of the city.

Apart from the building structures, pottery and marble building elements were investigated to examine the trade connections of Ainos. The pottery fine wares from late Hellenistic to the late Roman era show a constant import especially from workshops from Asia Minor from the 1st century BC to the 7th century AD and also from North Africa starting from the 2nd century AD.

The use of marble is noticeable from the Roman Imperial time onwards. The main source was the Proconnesus Island in the Sea of Marmara. The capitals, in particular, demonstrate that large-scale buildings were erected in Roman Imperial and early Byzantine times. This hints at the wealth of Ainos during these periods.

Image Credit

Fig. 1: © A. Cramer & Th. Schmidts, RGZM.

References

Alpar 2001

B. Alpar, Plio-Quaternary History of the Turkish Coastal Zone of the Enez-Evros Delta: NE Aegean Sea, Mediterranean Marine Science 2, 2001, 95–118.

Asdracha 1976

C. Asdracha, La région des Rhodopes aux XIIIe et XIVe siècles. Étude de géographie historique (Athens 1976).

Başaran 1999

S. Başaran, Zum Straßennetz um Ainos, in: P. Scherrer – H. Täuber – H. Thür (ed.), Steine und Wege. Festschrift Dieter Knibbe (Wien 1999) 343–348.

Başaran 2007

S. Başaran, Die Ausgrabungen in Ainos. Ein Überblick, in: A. Iakobidou (ed.), Thrace in the Graeco-Roman World. Proceedings of the 10th International Congress of Thracology. Komotini – Alexandroupolis 2005 (Athens 2007) 72–79.

Brückner et al. 2015

H. Brückner – Th. Schmidts – H. Bücherl – A. M. Seeliger, Zur Frage der Häfen von Ainos – eine Zwischenbilanz, in: Th. Schmidts – M. M. Vučetić (eds.), Häfen im 1. Millennium AD: bauliche Konzepte, herrschaftliche und religiöse Einflüsse. Interdisziplinäre Forschungen zu Häfen von der Römischen Kaiserzeit bis zum Mittelalter 1. RGZM Tagungen 22 (Mainz 2015) 53–76.

Danoff 1979

Der Kleine Pauli 1 (1979) 177 s. v. Ainos (Ch. Danoff).

Dumont 1892

A. Dumont, Mélanges d'archéologie et d'épigraphie (Paris 1892).

Hasluck 1908–1909

F. W. Hasluck, Monuments of the Gattelusi, BSA 15, 1908–1909, 249–257.

Karadima 2004

Ch. Karadima, Ainos: An Unknown Amphora Production Center in the Evros Delta, in: J. Eiring – J. Lund (ed.), Transport Amphorae and Trade in the Eastern Mediterranean, Acts of the International Colloquium at the Danish Institute at Athens, September 26–29/2002, Monographs of the Danish Institute at Athens 5 (Athens 2004) 155–161.

Kaygusuz 1986

I. Kaygusuz, Neue Inschriften aus Ainos (Enez), EpigrAnat 8, 1986, 65–70.

Kaygusuz – Erzen 1986

I. Kaygusuz – A. Erzen, Stempel auf Amphorenhenkeln aus Ainos (Enez), EpigrAnat 7, 1986, 7–16.

Ousterhout 1985

R. Ousterhout, The Byzantine Church at Enez. Problems in Twelfth-Century Architecture, JbÖByz 35, 1985, 261–280.

Ousterhout – Bakirtzis 2007

R. Ousterhout – Ch. Bakirtzis, The Byzantine Monuments of the Evros/Meric River Valley (Thessaloniki 2007).

Soustal 1991

P. Soustal, Thrakien (Thrake, Rodope und Haimimontos), Tabula Imperii Byzantini 6, DenkschrWien 221 (Wien 1991).

Tzochev 2010

Ch. Tzochev, Between the Black Sea and the Aegean. The Diffusion of Greek Trade Amphorae in Southern Thrace, in: K. Tezgor – N. Inaishvili (eds.), Patabs I – Production and Trade of Amphorae in the Black Sea (Istanbul 2010).

Wright 2014

C. Wright, The Gattilusi Lordships and the Aegean World 1355–1462 (Leiden 2014).

Exploring Rivers and Ancient Settlements in Aegean Thrace through Spatial Technology

Despoina Tsiafaki – Vasilis Evangelidis

Introduction: The River Geography of Thrace

Since the early civilizations, the rivers as dynamic carriers of natural and cultural forces had a deep impact on human landscapes.[1] Nevertheless, the ancient Greek civilization was never really a waterway culture since most of the rivers of mainland Greece were small, not navigable and quite often torrential in their character.[2] In sharp difference to the south, the geography of northern Greece and more specifically the Aegean Thrace (fig. 1),[3] is characterized by the presence of two major rivers:[4] Nestos to the west, and Evros to the east, the second largest river of the Eastern Europe with a total length of 515 km.[5]

To these large river systems, we should also add many tributaries flowing in the plain that extends between the modern regional centers of Xanthi and Komotini: Kompsatos, Kosynthos and Travos, all of which discharge in Vistonis Lake and Lissos in the Aegean Sea. These along with a considerable number of small creeks or torrential rivers that flow from the highlands of Rhodopi to the coastal area, shaped not only the physical but also the cultural landscape as ethnic, tribal or cultural boundaries in Aegean Thrace.

This was an area of significant importance not only for its physical variability in river landscapes but mostly as the meeting point of the Aegean world of the Greek city states (ἀποικίαι) with the inland cultures of various Thracian tribes like the Sapaians, Vistones or Kikones who inhabited the area (Hom 2.864; Hdt 7.110). A major development in the settlement pattern of the area (fig. 2) occurred in the early 7th century BC, when Greek -Ionian settlements begun to get established along the coast.[6] During the late Classical and early Hellenistic period the area became part of the Macedonian kingdom[7] and occasionally fell in the grasp of the various tribal Thracian rulers.[8] Later the official annexation (46 AD) of this large region to the Roman Empire[9] radically changed the existing settlement and urbanization framework with new cities being founded closer to the Via Egnatia, a major military and commercial road of the empire that crossed the area towards Byzantium.[10]

Scope of this project is to explore the impact of these large rivers on the local economy over time and how this is reflected on the spatial scale. Thus, our main research objectives seek to illustrate an overview of the region archaeologically in terms of settlement and economy and to investigate with the contribution of spatial technology (Open source GIS) how site placement relates to the wider environment. More specifically, we aim to explore to what extent the proximity to a river played a role as a criterion for the selection of a settlement to be established at. This is of great interest particularly in the case of the *apoikiai*, since it could contribute to a better knowledge and understanding of the decision strategy behind their foundation.

Fig. 1: The River and Wetland geography of Aegean Thrace.

To this direction the employment of open source GIS technology[11] (here the open and renewable QGSIS) with advantages like transparency of code, openness to public scrutiny, public availability, portability, transferability and support by a growing online community can provide the archaeological community with a research tool that with minimal effort and no costly private licenses can be available to anyone who is willing to phrase the appropriate questions over any set of data. What follows are some first observations and preliminary results from this ongoing project.

Fluvian Landscapes and Economic Perspectives

The importance of rivers and their adjacent fluvial landscapes as economic vectors – zones is without doubt immense.[12] Since navigability was clearly not the case with the rivers of Aegean Thrace (with the probable exception of the northern part of Evros[13]) any discussion about the economic role of the different river systems should focus primarily on their relationship with farming activities.[14] All accounts agree that the economy of the river valleys or of the great alluvial deltaic plains is underpinned by agriculture because of their natural fertility.[15] Consequently, the presence of large water bodies like the rivers Nestos and Evros along with their tributaries led to the logical

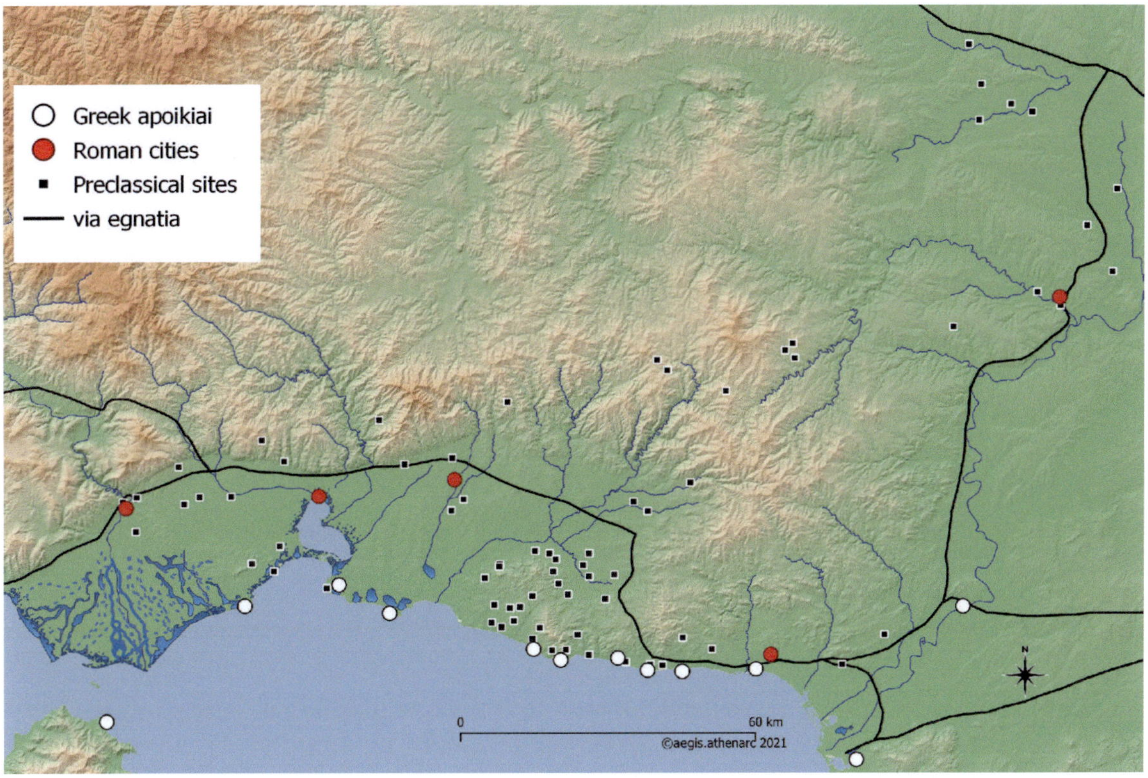

Fig. 2: Distribution of major sites in Aegean Thrace from the Late Iron Age to Roman times.

assumption that the economy of the area must have been in a great extent agricultural, fed by the ample provision of fresh water.[16] This is further supported by ancient sources like Pindar (Paean 2.25–26. 60), Diodorus Siculus (13.7.2) or Homer (Iliad 11.222) who mention the fertility of Thrace, which is characterised as εὔκαρπος and πολύδωρος.

Although river floodplains could be attractive for agricultural use there are undoubtedly many other factors (topography, altitude, rainfall) that must be considered to determine what type of economic activities took place on a certain area. Thus, a crucial point in our analysis of how this land was used in antiquity is to determine the amount of arable land and the quality of soils provided by the specific rivers.

Today the lands in the plain of Nestos, Lissos – Kompsatos and along the valley of Evros are heavily and densely cultivated but this might have not always been the case. The ancient landscape appears to be quite different due to many environmental variables and restraints. One of them was the presence of large areas of wetland (fig. 1) extending along the coast for over 100 km.[17] The system includes the Nestos Delta with the lagoons of Keramoti at the west, the Vistonis Lake[18] with the area of Porto Lagos in the middle and the Thracian Lagoons to the east. For the large area that stretches between Xanthi and Komotini, the semi-torrential rivers Kosynthos, Kompsatos and Travos that carry large amounts of fresh water from the mountains formed an extensive wetland.

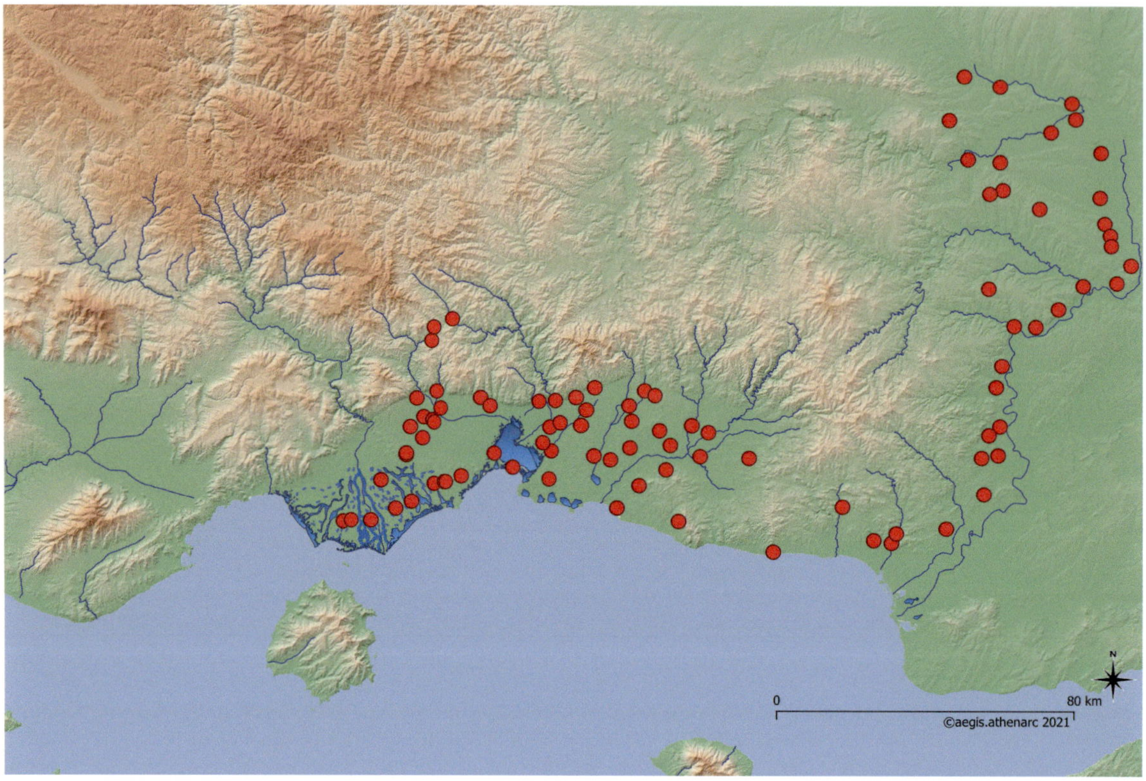

Fig. 3: Recorded Floods in Aegean Thrace (based on the 'Plan 12 Thrace Region Map' created by the Ministry of Environment, Energy and Climate Change, Special Secretariat for Water).

Wetlands[19] as such can encompass a wide range of different types of terrains, such as fens, bogs, marshes, swamps, shallow lakes (Chrysoupoli), or fresh or saltwater marshes like those forming the landscape around the current Lake Vistonis but also much of the coastal area near the Greek colony of Abdera (Lafri and Lafrouda sandunes). This type of areas can support vegetation adapted to the wet conditions (hydrophytes) but mostly are characterized by the absence of flooding-intolerant vegetation like cereals, which seem to constitute the basic cultivated crop in ancient farming societies. In such wetland areas, only low-intensity agricultural activities are expected but not the systematic farming that could sustain organized societies based primarily on agriculture. Similarly to wetlands large areas around the fresh water bodies were covered by riparian forests like that of Nestos known as "Kotza Orman" (Great Forest), which at the beginning of the 19th century covered approximately an area extending over 124.000 acres.[20]

The extensive wetlands, the riparian forests[21] in addition to flood-stricken zones (fig. 3) must have significantly limited the amount of land suitable for agriculture. Flood zones for instance were important determinants for settlement and farming. The violent character of flash flooding (typical for the secondary rivers of the area) was hazardous for agriculture while seasonal flooding as observed in the Evros sub-basin could have

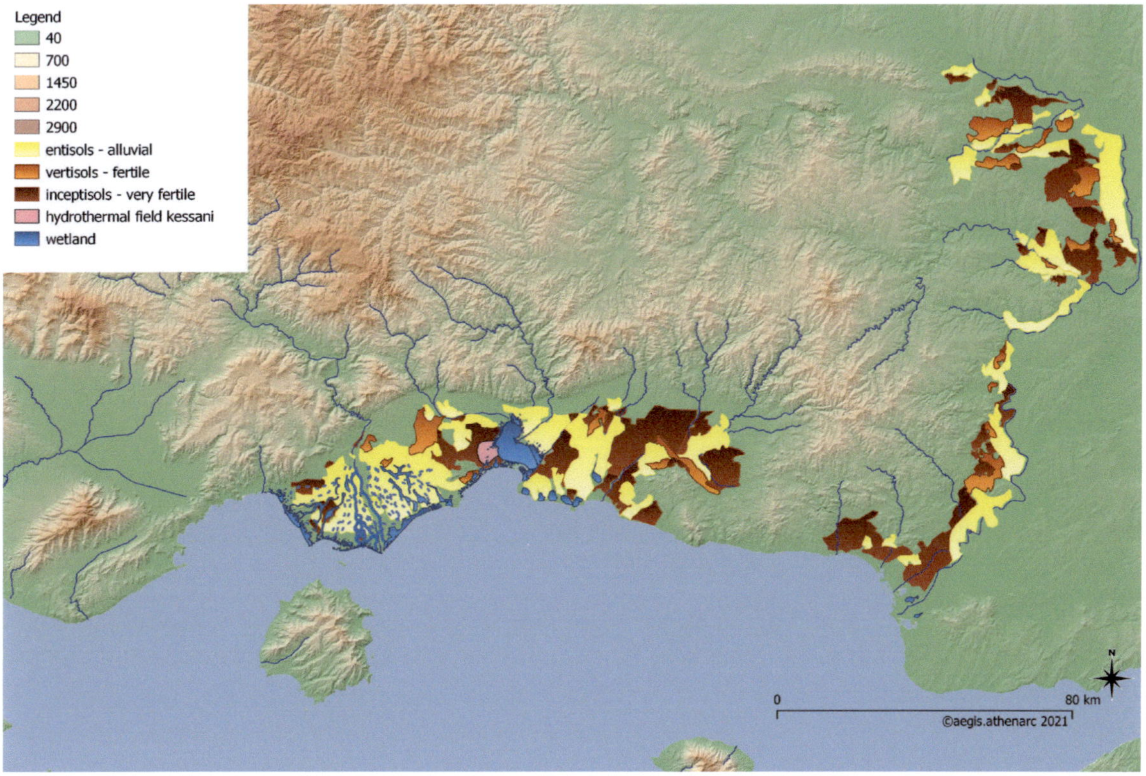

Fig. 4: Soil map of Aegean Thrace (based on soil map produced by the Aristotle University of Thessaloniki, School of Agriculture, Lab of Applied Soil Science).

seriously affected the existing schemes of land division as was the case until recently with Erythropotamos.[22]

To these environmental restraints we should add the quality of the soils.[23] The entisols, vertisols and inceptisols, which dominate the area (fig. 4),[24] are chiefly clay type soils that when saturated with water can go into peraquic condition.[25] Consequently, the heavy texture and unstable behavior of these soils makes it difficult for many crop and tree species to grow. In these soils, rain-fed farming can prove to be very difficult because vertisols and entisols can be worked only under a very narrow range of moisture conditions: they are very hard when dry and very sticky when wet.[26] This kind of soil because it is almost impermeable when saturated can be beneficiary for the cultivation of rice or kiwis (products of the modern local agriculture), but they are not suitable for basket feeders of agricultural societies like cereals (wheat, rye, barley).

Therefore, early agriculture in these fluvial landscapes could have been plagued by poor growing conditions. Moreover, despite the proximity to large water bodies many of the soils encountered in the region (especially around Komotini) are characterized by lack – as noticed by the original SPRP[27] (Survey Project of the Rhodopi Plain*)* survey of 1992 – of natural water resources, something that would have further hindered agricultural potentials.

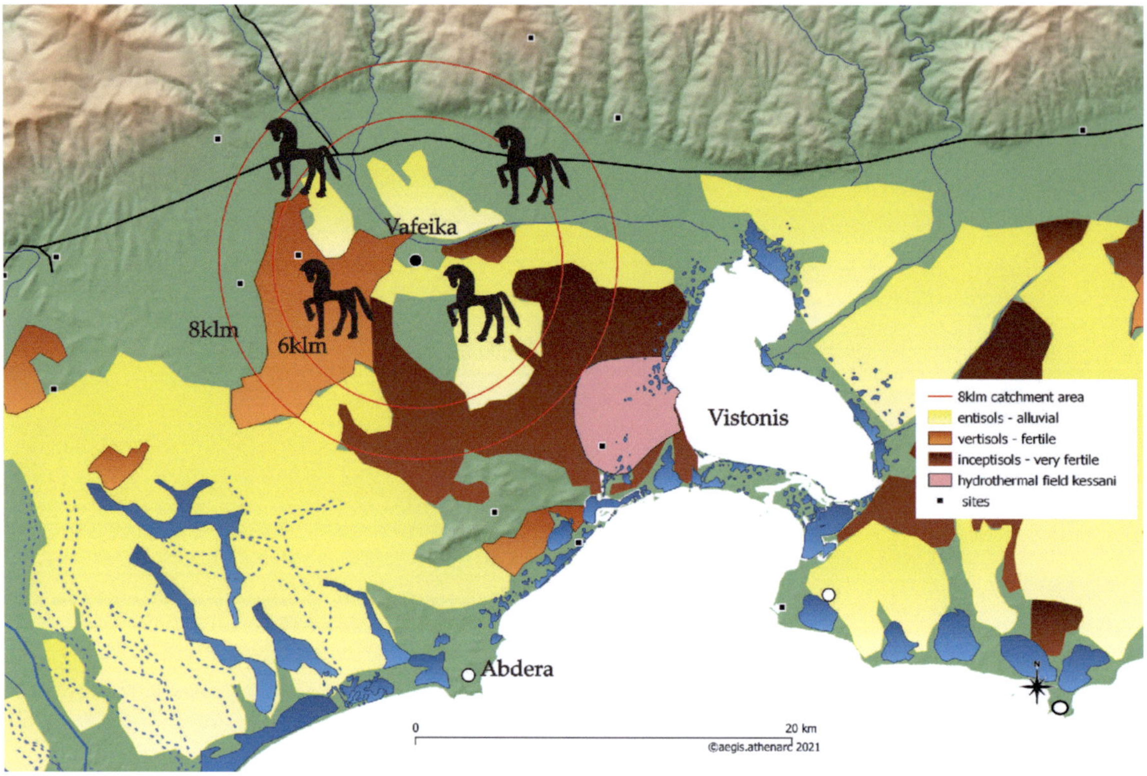

Fig. 5: The Vistonian heartland: 8 km buffer zone around the Early Thracian site discovered at Vafeika near the shores of River Kosynthos.

Nevertheless, the different micro areas,[28] clearly support a great variety of food producing activities besides cereal farming like river fisheries or hunting, which would have contributed significantly to the local economies. Most importantly the entisols, inceptisols and vertisols would have been perfect for cattle or other type of animal herding.[29] Aside from soil order, pastoral farming is more likely to be found in areas with cold strong winds and a wet climate and from this perspective the region is perfect since the prevailing north or northeast winds that dominate during the winter and summertime can reach speeds up to 8–9 Beauforts (60–70 km/h). All these conditions are more advantageous to raising livestock than crops. Therefore, we can envisage terrains that could have supported a pastoral type of economy based on large herds grazing on the extensive areas of grassland as is attested for the Vistones (fig. 5) who fed their horses in the waters of the river Kosynthos.[30]

In order to sum up we should keep in mind that the various accounts that see Thrace as a "granary" usually make general references to the extensive land, reaching Euxeinos Pontos to the east and river Danube to the north.[31] As for the Aegean Thrace though, it appears that there were serious environmental restraints, which, to a certain extent, were dictating the range of financial activities taking place here.[32] The important question is how these environmental restraints are reflected in the settlement patterns.

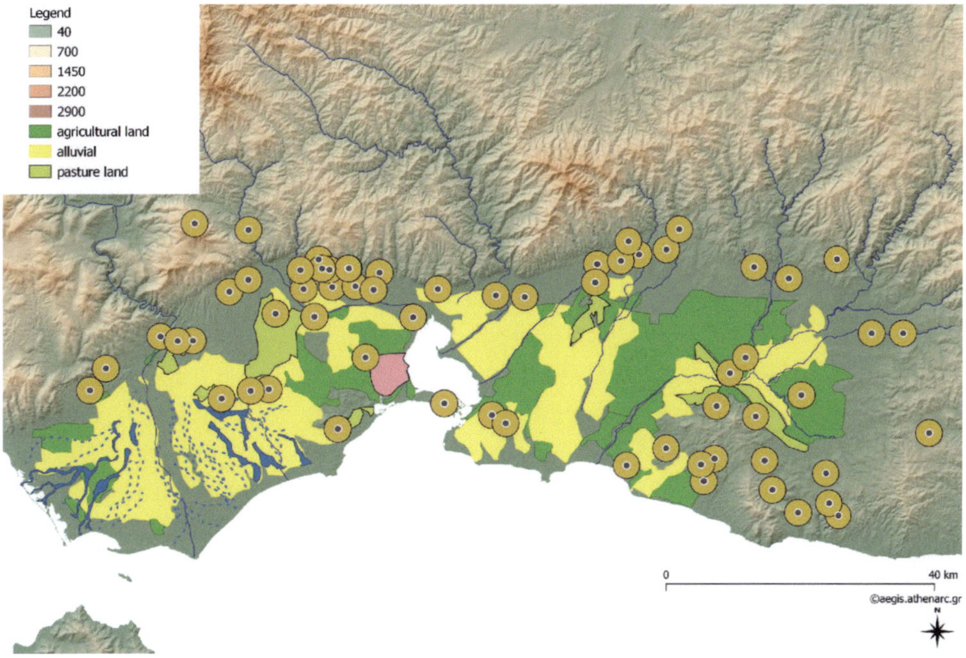

Fig. 6: Rural sites of Aegean Thrace with 2 km buffer zones (possible agricultural zones).

Environmental Restraints and Strategies of Settlements

A key observation regarding the settlement patterns of the region is the following: although it is commonly accepted that settlements are clustered near water bodies, the spatial data indicate that the largest concentration of urban (with some exceptions) and rural settlements is in a relative safe distance from major active rivers. The combination of river avulsion, frequent flooding, major shifts in the river courses and areas covered by swamps, riparian forests and wetlands would have made the broader Nestos and Northern Evros floodplain generally unsuitable for habitation.[33] Furthermore, the high-water table (characteristic for clay type soils like entisols[34]), the flat alluvial plains, and frequent flooding have the potential to expand the available breeding sites for the *Anopheles* mosquito, the major carrier of malaria.[35] The sites appear to clusters toward elevations in the landscape, mostly between 170–180 m. and 200 m. in the margins above the impact of flooding, river movements, poor drainage and mosquito zones. Localities such as the formation of the low hills that appear in the plain of modern Komotini area (the catchment area of Kompsatos) or the western bank of Evros would have provided protection from flooding thus allowing the development of rural settlements.[36]

To a great extent, knowledge about the settlement patterns of the local Thracian communities remains sporadic and limited.[37] The historical sources provide scant information and not always trustworthy. As elsewhere in Iron Age northern Greece, the settlements identified in western Rhodopi (like the Asar Tepe Ergane, Xylagane,

Sarakine, Toxotes) are mostly fortified sites in the elevated zones, which possibly controlled smaller rural settlements lying regularly in the foothills or in localities near the smaller rivers like Kosynthos.[38] In the lowlands many settlements reveal themselves as mounds standing above the flat country around them. Fortified *akropoleis* and rural settlements may represent the existence of many local economic and cultural units that were based on low intensity farming (normally in a range of 2 km around the settlement) and cattle herding (fig. 6). As aforementioned large tracts of land in the alluvial plain, especially in the area between Nestos River and the Vistonis Lake, had the profile of an extended grassland and thus were appropriate for cattle or animal herding. Since even small herds (of cattle and horses) require relatively large tracts of land (1.8 acre per cow), this would have reduced even further the amount of available arable land for systematic agriculture.[39]

The ancient sources like Herodotos[40] (5.6; 2.167.1) state that Thracians underrated agriculture. Clearly this can be received as an overstatement. Low intensity agriculture in short range from the settlements (fig. 6) was probably a very viable way for many tribal units to secure a successful living. Nevertheless, the lack of great urban agglomerations can be possibly seen as an indication that systematic agriculture on a massive scale was absent. On the other hand, the remarkable cluster of pre-Classical sites around the foot of Mount Ismaros (fig. 2) seems to be related mostly with the exploitation of the rich minerals rather than agriculture.

An interesting question that arises as an outcome of the results above is how the Greek colonies fit within this specific environmental and economical context. As aforementioned a common view concerning the colonization process here is that it was motivated by agrarian purposes.[41] The fertility of the region well attested by the ancient sources (Pindar 2.25–26), attracted the colonists who exploited the rich alluvial plains in expense of the local tribes. This seems to be the case of the Samothracian Peraia (Sale, Zone, Drys), which tried to secure the agricultural products that their island cities so desperately needed.[42] However, when the discussion comes to the larger cities such as Abdera and Maroneia,[43] the examination of spatial information leads to some interesting observations.

In sharp difference with Amphipolis and Ainos, at Strymon and the east bank of Evros respectively, which were founded to control navigable rivers, the relationship between the rest of the Greek colonies and the major rivers is small. Although Herodotos (7.126) describes how Nestos crosses the fields outside the walls of Abdera, the city was founded in the safest possible distance from the deltaic plain.[44] The predominant characteristic behind all colonial settlement (Abdera, Dikaia, Maroneia, Zone and Sale) along the flat surf-stricken coastline of Thrace was their location near good natural harbors, which admittedly is a rarity for the area. This emphasis on the sea and the need to secure and retain a safe link with the rest of the Greek world was such that in both Maroneia and Abdera, the building of new harbors was deemed necessary.[45]

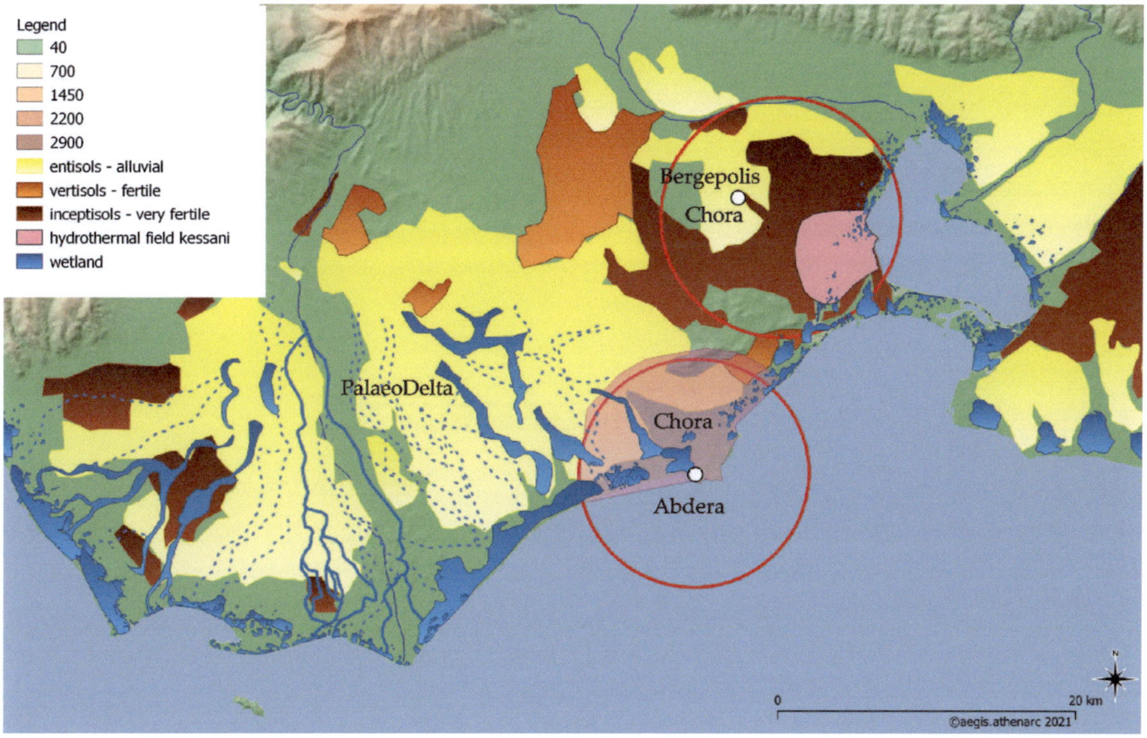

Fig. 7: Abdera and Bergepolis (Koutso) with 6 km buffer zones representing the ancient chora.

Whether these colonies – especially Abdera – were founded with a primary goal to exploit the alluvial plains remains unknown.[46] Undeniably views and theories about the geographic characteristics of these settlements seem to have been based on stereotypical models imported from other areas of the early Archaic Greek colonization like Magna Grecia[47] where the seek for fertile land was the main motive behind the colonial establishments. The *chora* of Abdera,[48] which originally did not exceed the mark line of the Thracian settlement at Mandra, the six-kilometer buffer area known from other Greek cities, included soils (and among them large areas of wetland) that could not support the necessary high-intensity cereal agriculture.

This probably justifies the foundation (sometime at the 5th century BC) of Bergepolis (fig. 7), a subsidiary city in the hinterland. Bergepolis, which is most probably identified with the remains of a settlement found in the modern village of Koutso (on the west bank of Vistonis),[49] is situated in the center of a zone dominated by incepticols soils that could – to a certain extent – have supported an intensive cereal crop production. The foundation of Bergepolis essentially doubled the rural chora of Abdera. Bergepolis as well as similar sites that were founded from Maroneia, such as Linos at the foot of Rodopi,[50] clearly shows the effort of the Greeks to establish themselves in the agricultural heart of the region away from the dangerous course of the great rivers.

However, this expansion, so necessary for the rural self-sufficiency of the population, took place at a later stage, when the cities had already acquired the power to maintain the stability that was necessary for the achievement of their rural objectives.

At the same time though it is worth noting that despite the control of the hinterland, the indigenous settlement structure remained essentially unaltered and many of the sites continued to exist throughout the Classical and Hellenistic era. This is a serious indication that the modes of economic exploitation in the area did not radically change.

Conclusions – Discussion

Already from 1992 the SPRP gave special emphasis to "*a persisting system of environmental conditions and human responses*". It is obvious that the environmental factors, in this case mainly the alluvial process and the existence of extensive fluvial landscapes, affected (directly or indirectly) the economy and the settlement patterns of the area. Naturally this is not something new or particularly groundbreaking. What is interesting in the case of the Aegean Thrace is the mingling of different cultural elements that compete for the same resources, while at the same time faced the same environmental challenges.

It is also clear that besides "life-givers" the large rivers dominating the region, created (due to a series of ecological restraints) large areas unsuitable for habitation or systematic exploitation. The most important restriction was the quality of the predominantly clay type soil that would certainly have limited the real agricultural potential of the area, especially in the large floodplains. These environmental factors combined with cultural constraints formed to a large extent the settlement patterns of the indigenous tribes.

Low intensity farming (characterized by low yield per hectare), little investment in land drainage and crops suited to specific regional conditions in conjunction with livestock breeding, which was favored by the terrain, was probably the dominant type of a mixed economy. This, we think, is reflected in the absence of great native urban agglomerations. The same environmental conditions must have affected to a certain extent the decision strategy and economy of the Greek coastal colonies. Undeniably the different environmental factors indicate the existence of many individual local economies, which developed within the well-defined geographical and environmental micro-zones. The Thracian settlements with the mountainous forts and the emphasis on animal herding and low intensity farming represent one group. The Greek trade colonies and their gradual expansion towards the interior with the clear aim to control land routes[51] and fertile land another. These were occasionally conflicting but, in many cases, they seem to have functioned reciprocally as the Maroneia case proves.

In conclusion we can say that the environmental factors like the extensive mosquito zones, the extensive riparian vegetation, the clay type soils or the extensive floods are factors that should be seriously considered when analyzing the economy and habitation of such culturally diverse area. If we go further, it becomes clear that the environmental reality quite often contributes significantly to the archaeological research.

Aknowledgements

The present work was supported by the project "Computational Science and Technologies: Data, Content and Interaction" / "Technologies for Content Analysis in Culture", MIS code 5002437, co-financed by Greece and European Union in the framework of the Operational Programme "Competitiveness, Entrepreneurship and Innovation" 2014–2020.

Notes

[1] Tilley 1994, 124–136; Strang 2004; Edgeworth 2011.

[2] Mariolakos 2017; Skoulikidis et al. 2017.

[3] Bouzek – Graninger 2015, 12–21.

[4] Skoulikidis et al. 2009, 421–466.

[5] Handrinos et al. 2005.

[6] Baralis 2008; Tiverios 2008.

[7] Isaac 1986; Hatzopoulos 1996, 186. 245 f.

[8] Archibald 1998; Delev 2018, 192 (on the late Odryssian kingdom).

[9] Loukopoulou 1987; Avramea 2003; Lozanov 2015, 75–90.

[10] Lolos 2007.

[11] Hodgkinson 2010; Orengo 2015, 64–82; Bibby – Ducke 2017

[12] Newson 1994; Tóth 2006. See the discussion in Franconi 2017.

[13] De Boer 2010.

[14] Zeder 2006; 2008; Zeder – Smith 2009.

[15] Brown 1997; Zeder – Smith 2009, 686.

[16] Casson 1968, 9 f.

[17] Gerakis 1992.

[18] Diamantis 1985; Babjimopoulos – Antonopoulos 1992.

[19] Palang et al. 2007.

[20] Papaioannou 1953.

[21] Verry et al. 2004.

[22] Koutsoyiannis et al. 2012.

[23] USDA 1975, (Vertisols 375) (Inceptisos 227) (Entisols 179).
[24] <https://esdac.jrc.ec.europa.eu/content/soil-map-east-macedonia-thrace-region-soil-textural-classification-map> (source ESDAC European Soil Data Center)
[25] Yassoglou et al. 2017, 71–85.
[26] Ehrmann et al. 2007.
[27] Efstratiou 1996; Efstratiou – Ammerman 2004; Ammerman et al. 2006.
[28] Efstratiou – Ammerman 1996.
[29] Mace – Houston 1989, 185–204; WISP 2007, 1–4.
[30] Triantaphyllos – Kallintzi 1998.
[31] Hom. Il. 11. 222; Pindar 2.25–26, 60.
[32] Ammerman et al. 2006.
[33] See generally Zeder 2006; 2008.
[34] USDA 179.
[35] Manguin 2013.
[36] Ammerman et al. 2006.
[37] Triantaphyllos 1987–1990; Baralis 2008, 114; Triantaphyllos 2009.
[38] Triantaphyllos 1990; Baralis 2008, 105–107; Matsas 2017a; Matsas 2017b; Kallintzi – Papadopoulos 2017; Triantaphyllos 2017.
[39] Ingold 1980; Mace – Houston 1989.
[40] Hdt 5.6: "The idler is most honored, the tiller of the soil most scorned; he is held in highest honor who lives by war and robbery" (transl. A. D. Godley 1922, Loeb Classical Library).
[41] Baralis 2008, 113 f.
[42] Tiverios 2008, 107–109.
[43] Karadima 2017.
[44] Isaac 1986, 72; Kallintzi 2011; Kallintzi 2017.
[45] Samiou 1999.
[46] Isaac 1986, 108 where he emphasizes the strategic role of the site and the prosperity as a result from the contact with the Thracians.
[47] Baralis 2008, 113.
[48] Kallintzi 2011.
[49] Tiverios 2008, 96.
[50] Baralis 2008, 120.
[51] Salviat 1999; Delev – Popov 2002; Palavestra 2007; De Boer 2010.

Image Credits

All images have been produced by QGIS version 2.18.3 with photo editing by noncommercial photo editing software.

References

Ammerman et al. 2006

A. J. Ammerman – N. Efstratiou – M. Ntinou – M. Michalakas, Εφαρμογές της „Αρχαιολογίας του Τοπίου" στη Θράκη. Τα πρώτα στοιχεία για τις πρώιμες Νεολιθικές εγκαταστάσεις στην περιοχή, AErgoMak 18, 2006, 1–8.

Archibald 1998

Z. H. Archibald, The Odrysian Kingdom of Thrace: Orpheus Unmasked (Oxford 1998).

Avramea 2003

A. Avramea, Thrace during the Roman Period, in Thrace 2 (Athens 2003) 135–150.

Babjimopoulos – Antonopoulos 1992

C. Babjimopoulos – V. Antonopoulos, Hydrological Review of Lake Vistonis, in: P. A. Gerakis (ed.), Conservation and Management of Greek Wetlands: Proceedings of a Greek Wetlands Workshop held in Thessaloniki 17–21 April 1989 (Thessaloniki 1992) 333–348.

Baralis 2008

A. Baralis, The Chora Formation of the Greek Cities of Aegean Thrace in: P. Guldager-Bilde – J. H. Petersen (eds.), Meetings of Cultures in the Black Sea Region: Between Conflict and Coexistence, Black Sea Studies 8 (Aarhus 2008) 101–130.

Bibby – Ducke 2017

D. Bibby – B. Ducke, Free and Open Source Software Development in Archaeology. Two Interrelated Case Studies: gvSIG CE and Survey2GIS, Internet Archaeology 43.

Bouzek – Graninger 2015

J. Bouzek – D. Graninger, Geography in: J. Valeva- E. Nankov- D. Graninger (eds.), A Companion to Ancient Thrace (London 2015) 12–21.

Brown 1997

A. G. Brown, Alluvial Geoarchaeology: Floodplain Archaeology and Environmental Change (Cambridge 1997).

Casson 1968

S. Casson, Macedonia, Thrace and Illyria (Groningen 1968).

De Boer 2010

J. G. de Boer, River Trade in Eastern and Central Thrace from the Bronze Age till the Hellenistic Period, Eirene 46, 2010, 176–189.

Delev 2018

P. Delev, Did a Late Odryssian Kingdom ever Exist?, in: Stephanos archaeologicos as 80 annum profesoris Ludmili Getov, Studia Archaeologica Universitatis Serdicensis Suppl. 6 (Sofia 2018) 191–196.

Delev – Popov 2002

P. Delev – H. Popov, The Ancient Road Network in the Middle Mesta Region, in: A. Bozkova – P. Delev (eds.), Koprivlen 1: Rescue Archaeological Investigations along the Gotse Delchev-Drama Road 1998–1999 (Sofia 2002) 57–62.

Diamantis 1985
P. Diamantis, Hydrogeological Study of the Vistonis Lake Area (Athens 1985).

Edgeworth 2011
M. Edgeworth (ed.), Fluid Pasts: Archaeology of Flow (Bristol 2011).

Efstratiou – Ammerman 1996
N. Efstratiou – A. J. Ammerman, Τα πρώτα ευρήματα της παλαιολιθικής εποχής στη Θράκη, Archaeologia 60, 1996, 7–12.

Efstratiou – Ammerman 2004
N. Efstratiou – A. J. Ammerman, Survey in Aegean Thrace: Exploring the Landscape, Archaeological Field Survey in Cyprus: Past History, Future Potentials, British School at Athens Studies 11 (Athens 2004) 183–190.

Efstratiou 1996
N. Efstratiou, New Investigations in Thrace, in: E. Alram-Stern (ed.), Die Ägäische Frühzeit 2, 1: Das Neolithikum in Griechenland, mit Ausnahme von Kreta und Zypern (Wien 1996) 576–580.

Ehrmann et al. 2007
W. Ehrmann – G. Schmiedl – Y. Hamann – T. Kuhnt – C. Hemleben – W. Siebel, Clay Minerals in Late Glacial and Holocene Sediments of the Northern and Southern Aegean Sea,. Palaeogeography, Palaeoclimatology, Palaeoecology 249, 2007, 36–57.

Franconi 2017
T. V. Franconi (ed.), Fluvial Landscapes in the Roman World, JRA Suppl. 104 (Portsmouth 2017).

Gerakis 1992
P. A. Gerakis (ed.), Conservation and Management of Greek Wetlands: Proceedings of a Greek Wetlands Workshop held in Thessaloniki 17–21 April 1989 (Thessaloniki 1992) 333–428.

Handrinos et al. 2005
G. Handrinos – A. Athanasiadis – Y. Rigas, Evros Delta. Princess of Thrace's Nature (Athens 2005).

Hatzopoulos 1996
M. B. Hatzopoulos, Macedonian Institutions under the Kings. A Historical and Epigraphical Study, Meletemata 22 (Athens 1996).

Hodgkinson 2010
A. K. Hodgkinson, Open Source Survey and GIS Manual, Documentation. Oxford Archaeology, <http://library.thehumanjourney.net/367> (last access: 12th August 2019).

Ingold 1980
T. Ingold, Hunters, Pastoralists and Ranchers (Cambridge 1980).

Isaac 1986
B. Isaac, The Greek Settlements in Thrace until the Macedonian Conquest (Leiden 1986).

Kallintzi 2011
C. S. Kallintzi, Η χώρα των Αβδήρων. Συμβολή στην αρχαιολογία και ιστορική τοπογραφία του νότιου τμήματος του Νομού Ξάνθης. (Ph. D. diss. University of Thessaly, Volos 2011) <http://thesis.ekt.gr/thesisBookReader/id/31737#page/ 1/mode/2up, and, http://hdl.handle.net/10442/hedi/31737> (last access: 12th August 2019).

Kallintzi 2017
C. S. Kallintzi, Άβδηρα, in: Vlachopoulos – Tsiafaki 2017, 498–501.
Kallintzi – Papadopoulos 2017
K. Kallintzi – S. Papadopoulos, Νομός Ξάνθης. Προϊστορικοί χρόνοι in: Vlachopoulos – Tsiafaki 2017, 488–492.
Karadima 2017
Chr. Karadima, Μαρώνεια, in: Vlachopoulos – Tsiafaki 2017, 518–521.
Koutsoyiannis et al. 2012
D. Koutsoyiannis – N. Mamassis – A. Efstratiadis – N. Zarkadoulas – Y. Markonis, Floods in Greece, in: Z. W. Kundzewicz (ed.), Changes of Flood Risk in Europe (Wallingford 2012) 238–256.
Lolos 2007
Y. Lolos, Via Egnatia after Egnatius: Imperial Policy and Inter-regional Contacts, Mediterranean Historical Review 22, 2007, 273–293.
Loukopoulou 1987
L. Loukopoulou, Provinciae Macedoniae Finis Orientalis: The Establishment of the Eastern Frontier, in: Meletemata 3 – Two Studies in Ancient Macedonian Topography (Athens 1987) 64–112.
Lozanov 2015
I. Lozanov, Roman Thrace, in: J. Valeva – E. Nankov – D. Graninger (eds.), A Companion to Ancient Thrace (London 2015) 75–90.
Mace – Houston 1989
R. Mace – A. Houston, Pastoral Strategies for Survival in Unpredictable Environments: a Model of Herd Composition that Maximize Household Viability, Agricultural Systems 31, 1989, 185–204.
Manguin 2013
S. Manguin (ed.), Anopheles Mosquitoes. New Insights into Malaria Vectors (Croatia 2013).
Mariolakos 2017
I. Mariolakos, Ancient Greece and Water – Climatic Changes, Extreme Events, Water Management, and Rivers in Ancient Greece, in: Skoulikidis et al. 2017, 3–31.
Matsas 2017a
D. Matsas, Θράκη. Προϊστορικοί χρόνοι, in: Vlachopoulos – Tsiafaki 2017, 474–480.
Matsas 2017b
D. Matsas, Νομός Ροδόπης. Προϊστορικοί χρόνοι, in: Vlachopoulos – Tsiafaki 2017, 506–511.
Newson 1994
M. Newson, Hydrology and the River Environment (Oxford 1994).
Orengo 2015
H. A. Orengo, Open Source GIS and Geospatial Software in Archaeology: Towards their Integration into Everyday Archaeological Practice, in: A. T. Wilson – B. Edwards (eds.), Open Source Archaeology Ethics and Practice (Leiden 2015) 64–82.
Palang et al. 2007
H. Palang – H. Soovali – A. Printsmann, (eds.), Seasonal Landscapes (Springer 2007).

Palavestra 2007

A. Palavestra, Was there an Amber Route?, in: I. Galanakis (ed.) Between the Aegean and Baltic Seas – Prehistory across the Borders, Aegaeum 27 (Liege 2007) 349–355.

Papaioannou 1953

I. Papaioannou, Το δάσος του Κοτζά-Ορμάν, Ekloge (Reprinted in Thracian Chronicles 88), 1953, 167–170.

Salviat 1999

F. Salviat, Le roi Kersobleptos, Maronie, Apollonia, Thasos, Pistiros et l'histoire d'Herodote, BCH, 123, 1999, 259–273.

Samiou 1999

C. Samiou, Ancient Ports of Abdera in Aegean Thrace, in: H. Tzallas (ed.), 5th International Symposium on Ship Construction in Antiquity. Tropis 5: Nauplia, 26–28 August 1993 (Athens 1999) 363–368.

Skoulikidis et al. 2009

N. Skoulikidis – S. Zogaris – A. Economou – K. Gritzalis, The Rivers of the Balkans in: K. Tockner – U. Uehlinger – C. T. Robinson (eds.), Rivers of Europe (London 2009) 421–466.

Skoulikidis et al. 2017

N. Skoulikidis – E. Dimitriou – I. Karaouzas (eds.), The Rivers of Greece. Evolution, Current Status and Perspectives (Berlin 2017).

Strang 2004

V. Strang, The Meaning of Water (Oxford 2004).

Tilley 1994

C. Tilley, A Phenomenology of Landscape: Places, Paths and Monuments (Oxford 1994).

Tiverios 2008

M. Tiverios, Greek Colonization of the Northern Aegean in Greek Colonisation: An Account of Greek Colonies and Other Settlements Overseas, in: G. R. Tsetskhladze (ed.), Greek Colonisation. An Account of Greek Colonies and Other Settlements Overseas 2 (Leiden 2008) 1–154.

Tóth 2006

J. A. Tóth, River Archaeology, a New Field of Research. New Technologies in Archeology, International Symposium, Hungarian National Museum 2005, Archeometriai Műhely 1, 2006, 61–66 <http://www.ace.hu/am> (last access: 12th August 2019).

Triantaphyllos 1987–1990

D. Triantafyllos, Η Θράκη του Αιγαίου πριν από τον ελληνικό αποικισμό, Θρακική Επετηρίδα 7, 1987–1990, 298–312.

Triantaphyllos 1990

D. Triantaphyllos, Οχυρωματικοί περίβολοι στην ενδοχώρα της Αιγαιακής Θράκης, in: H. Koukouli – Chryssanthaki – O. Picard – T. Petrides (eds.), Μνήμη Δ. Λαζαρίδη. Πόλις και Χώρα στην αρχαία Μακεδονία και Θράκη, Proceedings of an Archaeological Conference Kavala 9–11 May 1986 (Thessaloniki 1990) 683–691.

Triantaphyllos 2009

D. Triantaphyllos, Η Θράκη από το Νέστο ως τον Έβρο πριν και μετά τον ελληνικό αποικισμό, in: Z.I . Bonias – J. Y. Perreault (eds.), Greeks and Thracians in Coastal and Inland Thrace during the

Years before and after the Great Colonization, Proceedings of the International Symposium, Thasos, 26–27 September 2008 (Thasos 2009) 187–204.

Triantaphyllos 2017

D. Triantaphyllos, Θράκη. Ιστορικοί Χρόνοι, in: Vlachopoulos – Tsiafaki 2017, 481–485.

Triantaphyllos – Kallintzi 1998

D. Triantaphyllos – K. Kallintzi, Αρχαιολογικά ευρήματα στον Κόσσυνθο της Ξάνθης, AErgoMak 12, 1998, 1–18.

USDA 1975

Soil Taxonomy. A Basic System of Soil Classification for making and Interpreting Soil Surveys, Agriculture Handbook no. 436: (Vertisols 375) (Inceptisos 227) (Entisols 179).

Verry et al. 2004

E. S. Verry – C. A. Dolloff – M. E. Manning, Riparian Ecotonea Functional Definition and Delineation for Resource Assessment, Water, Air, and Soil Pollution 4, 2004, 67–94.

Vlachopoulos – Tsiafaki 2017

A. Vlachopoulos – D. Tsiafaki (eds.), Αρχαιολογία. Μακεδονία Θράκη (Athens 2017).

WISP 2007

World Initiative for Sustainable Pastoralism (WISP), Pastoralists' Species and Ecosystems Knowledge as the Basis for Land Management. WISP Policy Brief 5, 2007, 1–4.

Yassoglou et al. 2017

N. Yassoglou – C. Tsadilas – C. Kosmas, Specific Characteristics of Alluvial Soils, in: N. Yassoglou – C. Tsadilas – C. Kosmas (eds.), The Soils of Greece. World Soils Book Series (Springer 2017) 71–85.

Zeder 2006

M. A. Zeder, Central Questions in the Domestication of Plants and Animals, Evolutionary Anthropology 15, 2006, 105–117.

Zeder 2008

M. A. Zeder, Domestication and Early Agriculture in the Mediterranean Basin: Origins, Diffusion, and Impact, in: Proceedings of the National Academy of Sciences of the United States of America 105, 2008, 11597–11604.

Zeder – Smith 2009

M. A. Zeder – B. D. Smith, A Conversation on Agricultural Origins, Current Archaeology 50, 2009, 681–691.

B. River Valleys and Regional Economies

River Valleys and Regional Economies: Introduction

Eurydice Kefalidou

The topics of this panel discuss the regional economies of three river valleys in two different areas: Athens and Attica with the Ilissos River; and northeastern Italy with the rivers that flow in the areas of Verona and Parma, respectively.

The Ilissos valley has been one of the most interesting places of Athens and Attica, not only because it was connected with several myths and cults but also because the use of its riverbanks seems to change through time as shown in the extensive summary by D. Di Giuliomaria, which covers a wide chronological framework, from the 6th century BC to the 8th century AD.

The other two rivers flow south of the Italian Alps, in today's Emilia-Romagna region. The paper of A. Mosca examines the distribution of settlements in the upper section of the Adige Valley, north of Verona, with a focus on the Roman era. It becomes clear that River Adige, the second largest river of Italy (it originates on the Alps, in the border between Italy, Austria and Switzerland) had a strong impact on the organization of habitation areas and on the agro-silvo-pastoral production while it had also been used for the transport of goods from the Adriatic ports to the hinterland.

The last paper, by A. R. Marchi and I. Serchia, is based on the results of recent excavations in the urban area of the Roman city of Parma, just next to the Parma Creek, a large stream, which is one of the more than 140 tributaries of River Po, the largest river in Italy. The excavations revealed a series of floods that caused damages and restorations to several structures from the Republican era to the Late Antiquity, when a strong flood led the creek to move towards the town and caused the need of constructing new walls to bar the water. Later (12th century) another strong flood caused a further displacement of the watercourse into its modern bed.

Walking Along the Ilissos River: Topographical Remarks about an Athenian District

Desirè Di Giuliomaria

The Ilissos valley under the plateau of Olympieion has always been one of the most fascinating places in Athens because of the several cults and myths mentioned in ancient literature and archaeological data, which confirm this most of the time (fig. 1).[1] The present study begun from two main questions: How did the areas around the Ilissos river change during time and how much did the abundance or scarcity of water influenced those changing processes. The Ilissos valley has been inhabited from the proto-Helladic to the Byzantine period, going through many changes of use.[2]

Starting as a necropolis area, it became one of the most important sacral places during the late Archaic period.[3] In the middle of 5th century BC, the area came through its first monumental phase, when the peripteral temple of Apollo in Doric order was built, as testified by archaeological data and epigraphic evidence on pottery (graffiti) found there[4]. Besides the sacral purpose of the area, the water affordability became the main productive resource for the development of workshops along the river. An inscription not found *in situ*, in the modern quarter of Plaka, and coming not so far away from the riverbanks, testifies a leather workshop nearby the Ilissos river around the second half of 5th century BC.[5] Workshops along watercourses should have existed since the Classical period in Athens, as some evidence along the Eridanos river and the ancient Agora testify.[6] In the Hellenistic period, the Ilissos valley became a peripheral residential district[7] until Roman times when Emperor Hadrian renewed the area and readdressed it to a sacral value. In the Byzantine time, however, the area developed into an operating centre of metallurgy and oil production supplying the entire city.[8]

Thanks to the Ephorate of Antiquities and the Archeologiki Etaireia of Athens, I had the possibility to study the excavation notebooks and the drawings realised by I. Threpsiadis and I. Travlos at the Ilissos valley between 1960 and 1967.[9] Therefore, I was able to explore the changes of the area's uses and topography.[10] The participation at the AIAC Congress in Bonn was fruitful due to the feedback that my paper received on the issues of Landscape Archaeology and productivity along rivers and water basins.

In any case, my research on the Ilissos valley is not complete; reading the documentation of the old excavation is only the first step. Consecutively, it requires to analyse the findings in the whole and to proceed to new surveys, in order to delineate the evolution of the area during the time clearer.

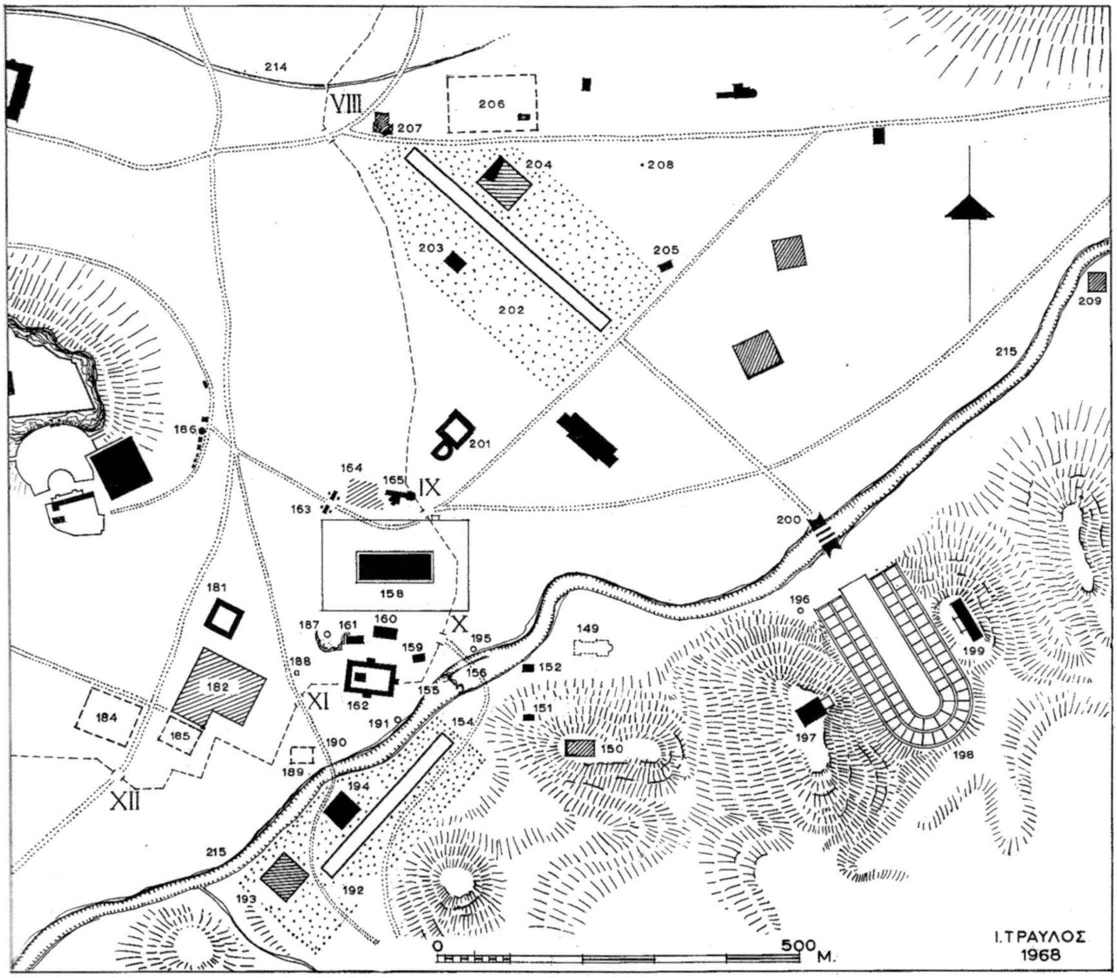

150. Heiligtum des Poseidon Helikonios
151. Artemis Agrotera
152. Metroon in Agrai
154. Relief des Pan
155. Kallirrhoe
156. Ilissos-Übergang
158. Olympieion
159. Kronos und Rhea
160. Apollon Delphinios
161. Gerichtsstätte am Delphinion
162. Panhellenion
163. Hadriansbogen
164. Häuser
165. Römisches Bad I
181. Gerichtsstätte am Palladion
182. Heiligtum des Kodros
184. Dionysion ἐν Λίμναις
185. Taureas-Palästra
186. Lysikrates-Denkmal
187. Heiligtum der Olympischen Ge
188. Amazonenstele
189. Pythion
190. Aphrodite in den Gärten
191. Altar der Ilissischen Musen
192. Kynosarges
193. Gymnasium
194. Gymnasium
195. Heiligtum des Boreas
196. Heiligtum des Pan, des Acheloos und der Nymphen
197. Tempel der Tyche
198. Stadion
199. Grabbau des Herodes Atticus
200. Brücke aus römischer Zeit
201. Römisches Gebäude mit halbkreisförmiger Halle
202. Lykeion
203. Lykeion-Bad
204. Gymnasium
205. Tempelfundamente
206. Gärten des Theophrast
207. Bad des Diochares
208. Grab des Nisos
209. Herakles Pankrates
214. Eridanos
215. Ilissos

Fig. 1: Plan of the Ilissos valley.

Notes

[1] Paus. 1.19.1–6.
[2] Threpsiadis – Travlos 1961; Pantelidou 1975, 113–115. 148–153; see also Marchiandi 2011.
[3] Thuc. 2.15, 3–6.
[4] Mitsos 1947; IG I3 948; see also Matthaiou 2011 and Asimakopoulou-Lintzeri et al. 2012–2013.
[5] IG I3 257.
[6] Bossolino – Di Giuliomaria 2015.
[7] Is. VIII 35.
[8] Kyriakou 2007.
[9] Preliminary excavation reports in Threpsiadis – Travlos 1961; Travlos 1971.
[10] The results will be published in the *Archeologiki Ephemeris* journal.

Image Credits

Fig. 1: Travlos 1971, 291, fig. 379.

References

Asimakopoulou-Lintzeri et al. 2012–2013
S. Asimakopoulou-Lintzeri – A. Makri – E. Sioumpara, Ανάγλυφο Λητούς και δύο χορηγικά μνημεία από την περιοχή νοτιοδυτικά του Ολυμπιείου. Συμβολή στην τοπογραφία των Αθηνών, ADelt 67–68, 2012–2013, A, 409–426.

Bossolino – Di Giuliomaria 2015
I. Bossolino – D. Di Giuliomaria, Conciatori e ciabattini nell'Atene classica: un approccio topografico, in: Dromoi, Studi sul mondo antico offerti a Emanuele Greco dagli allievi della Scuola Archeologica Italiana di Atene (Paestum 2015) 347–361.

Kyriakou 2007
D. Kyriakou, Το Ολυμπιείον και η ευρύτερη περιοχή (Athens 2007).

Marchiandi 2011
D. Marchiandi, L'area meridionale della città e la valle dell'Ilisso, in: E. Greco (ed.), Topografia di Atene. Sviluppo urbano e monumenti dalle origini al III sec. d. C. (Athens 2011) 369–396.

Matthaiou 2011
A.P. Matthaiouυ, Το Πύθιον παρά τον Ιλισσόν, in: A. Delivorrias – G. Despinis – A. Zarkadas (eds.), Έπαινος Luigi Beschi (Athens 2011) 259–271.

Mitsos 1947
M.Th. Mitsos, Inscription from Athens, Hesperia 16, 1947, 262–266.

Pantelidou 1975
M. Pantelidou, Αι προϊστορικαί Αθήναι (Athens 1975).
Threpsiadis – Travlos 1961
I. Threpsiadis – I. Travlos, Ανασκαφαί νοτίως του Ολυμπιείου (1961), ADelt 17, 1961, B, 9–14.
Travlos 1971
J. Travlos, Bildlexikon zur Topographie des antiken Athen (Tübingen 1971).

An Ancient Landscape Shaped by the River: The Impact of the Adige at the Base of the Alps. A New Research Perspective

Annapaola Mosca

The goal of this study is to analyze the impact of the upper section of the Adige at the base of the Alps on the ancient landscape and the economy with a focus on the Roman Age.[1]

The Settlement Pattern in the Adige Valley in Antiquity

How was the ancient course of the Adige river? It was very different from the current one and it must have influenced the settlement pattern in the entire valley. The river was probably larger and characterized by meanders, as we can see through aerial photographs and as ancient settlements seem to demonstrate. It is sometimes difficult to imagine environmental situations that have helped to define the ancient settlement organization, much more linked to the Adige river than today. Not only the Adige but also its tributaries have changed their course over the centuries, up to major changes between the 19th and the 20th century.[2] But only maps of the 19th century can attest with more precision how the Adige was before the adjustments and the construction of the railway in the second half of the19th century (1867).[3]

The river seems to have already influenced settlement patterns in pre-Roman periods. For example, if we consider the pre-Roman sites from south to north in the middle Val Lagarina, Castel Tierno, Castel Pradaglia (right bank) and Dosso Alto near Borgo Sacco (left bank) in the Bronze Age, we will see that they were located to control the Adige river south of Rovereto[4] while Nomi Cef (right bank) was in a marsh, along the river, south of the modern town of Rovereto in a strategic position, as perhaps the river was a commercial way, but also the river itself or the valley bottom could have been practicable by enemies.[5] Other settlements had the function of controlling the Adige Valley too, for example some sites scattered above the hills near the modern town of Trento[6] and "Dosson di Faedo".[7] Vadena/Pfatten between the modern cities of Trento and Bolzano was recognized as a commercial *emporium* on the river Adige.[8]

The Adige Valley has been used as a commercial route from the Adriatic ports since the pre-Roman period. Different data suggest that goods could arrive directly from the Adriatic ports but neither remains of pre-Roman or Roman boats nor ancient harbors have been identified so far in the upper part of the river. Moreover, the ancient written sources do not mention the practice of navigation along the Adige at the base of the Alps. It was assumed that from the end of the 6th until the early 4th century BC the wine, which arrived inside Greek amphorae via transmarine trade, was poured into wooden

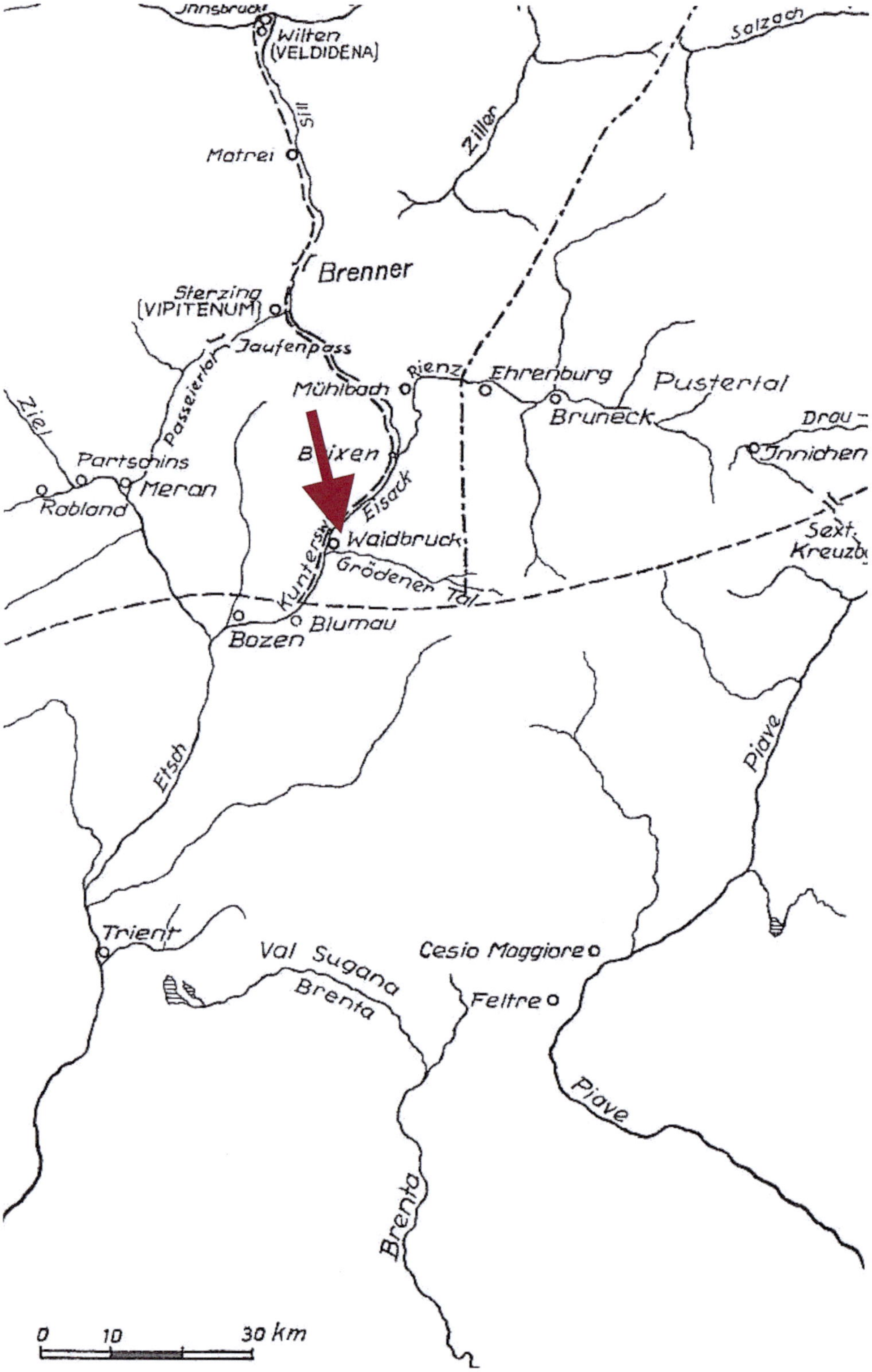

Fig. 1: Location of the Ponte Gardena / Waidbruck *statio*.

barrels to be transported in the Alpine valleys. This theory was based on the fact that in the area of *Mantua* (Forcello), which was a sort of strategic hub where the waterways met the paths from the Appennines and the paths and the waterways from the Alps, many amphorae from the Aegean area have been found.[9]

Several archaeological artefacts have shown a close relationship with the northern Adriatic area. This was demonstrated in the past with the discovery of artefacts from the Northern Adriatic area in Vadena/Pfatten along the Adige course.[10] The discovery in Settequerce/Siebeneich, in the Terlano/Terlan area, along the ancient course of the Adige river, of an Iron Age settlement with a place dedicated to worship with pottery artefacts of 5th–4th century BC very similar to those discovered in Este, led to the presumption of a direct connection with the Adriatic ports; the importance of the port of Adria in the Northern Adriatic area has been revalued, in connection to the possibility of transport along the river Adige.[11]

In the last period of the Roman Republic, exchanges between the population living at the base of the Alps and the Roman world increased, as we can deduce above all from the coins found in some settlements, for example in Laives/Leifers, along the river.[12] Probable drainage works made by stones along the Adige Valley, at the current state of research have been identified in Laives/Leifers dating back to the 4th century BC and prove that the Adige tended to overflow towards the settlement located on the conoids and in Vadena/Pfatten.[13] Here we can believe that this arrangement of pre-Roman settlements makes clear the close link with the river, since the settlements needed to be located near the river and not in a safer position.

The Impact between Local Populations and the Romans

This area, mainly connected to the Roman town of *Tridentum*, is generally supposed to have become part of the Roman world in the early Imperial period. We have a few literary sources about this territory in the first Roman Imperial era.

Perhaps the war between the Romans and the local population at the base of the Alps was not so bloody as reported by Horace.[14] Archaeological data indeed seem to suggest a gradual transition as shown by the flow of goods from the Mediterranean area[15] and as evidenced by the archaeological excavations in the current state of research.[16] The Alps did not mark the border of Italy as today but the border of the Italic regions of Augustus had to be on the southern base of the Alps.[17]

The reorganization of the territories at the base of the Alps led to the creation and strengthening of the urban center of *Tridentum* that probably played a decisive role already in the phases of the Roman conquest and must have taken place over several years, as attested by the milestone found in Val Venosta/Vintschgau, and by the edict of Claudius found in Val di Non.[18] When, during the 1st century AD, the emperors of the Flavian dynasty and their successors extended the fortifications along the *limes*

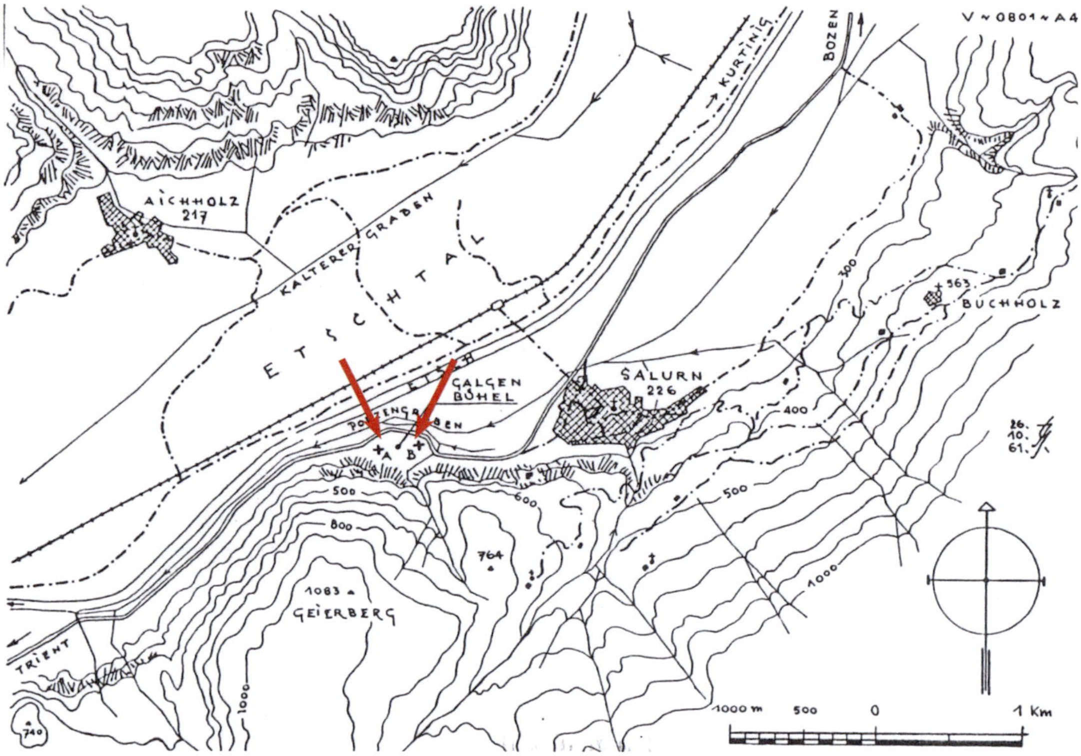

Fig. 2: Location of the Roman necropolis of Salorno.

of *Germania* and *Raetia*, the district became more intensely a territory of passage of armies and traders, but the archaeological data show that the district kept its own characteristics.[19]

Reorganization of the Settlement

For the Roman reorganization of the settlement, the river must have played an important role, as the city of *Tridentum*, probably founded in the second half of the 1st century BC[20], was built in close connection to the river and in the age of Augustus became the main center (*municipium*) of this district,[21] as we can deduce from the monumental remains of the Roman town, even if a Roman port has not yet been identified.[22]

The roads with their stations (*stationes*) together with the rivers marked the boundaries between the Italian territory and the neighboring provinces. Near the borders the custom stations have been set up. These *stationes* are mentioned in epigraphic sources; but these sources are later than the period when the duty stations may have been placed in key positions.[23] One has been identified in the area of Tel/Töll (which refers to the word *Telonium*) and was identified as *statio Miensis*.[24] The other one must have been located in the area of Colma/Kolmann – Ponte Gardena /Waidbruck along the course of the Isarco, a tributary of the Adige river, and on the main road that led to the Brenner pass, presumably already in the territory of the *Noricum* (fig. 1). This was the custom statio included in the district of the *Publicum Portorium Illyrici.*[25]

Local people were probably living in typical houses (built by wood and local stones without mortar), while artefacts had to come more massively from the Roman world, as has been noted in Settequerce/Siebeneich, along the upper river course.[26] Villages had necessarily been rebuilt in the same place closely connected to the river, e.g. Laives/ Leivers, on the left bank of the river, [27] probably where it was possible to cross the Adige; indeed, in Vaden/Pfatten, on the right bank of the river in front of Laives, a continuous settlement is attested.[28]

Only some buildings are distinguished as they were built with the use of lime mortar and with Roman imperial tiles. From north to south, on the left bank of the Adige, for example in Laives/Leifers – San Giacomo/St. Jakob, in a building built in the early Roman Imperial period, Roman *tegulae* (also with stamps) were found used in foundations; their purpose was probably to limit water infiltration since the building was in a marshy area near the river. This building had a short life, as it was destroyed by the flooding of the river. Judging from the recovered artefacts it had to be important and it was connected to a road and to the river [29]. In another building (1st–3rd century AD), identified as a *mansio*, many tiles have been found with a variant of *AVRESIS* stamp (fig. 3).[30] In Laghetti/Laag, in close contact with the river, there were buildings of considerable importance (1st–6th century AD). Excavations have led to recognize tiles with stamps *AVRESIS*, *LOCEIAVRESIS* and *CRVT* with variants and *tubuli* for the heating system. Artefacts from medium to large scale trade (Italic terra sigillata; amphorae similar to Dressel 6 B, but also sigillata and glass from the Rhine area and African red slip ware) have been identified in these buildings.[31]

In Villa/Vill of Egna/Neumarkt (left bank of the Adige (fig. 5), in the 1st century AD, a man who was linked to the Roman culture, judging by the choice of the iconographic motifs of his funerary stele, even if performed by a rough craftsman, had to inhabit there with his family (fig. 4); in the same village, late Roman republican *denarii* and imperial coins were recovered;[32] also, in the area around the medieval church of the modern village ancient artefacts are still reused.

Some villages located not far from the river have become important in the 2nd century AD, probably in relation to the importance acquired by the district that is increasingly functional to the needs of the *limes.* For example, in the 2nd century AD the village of Mezzocorona Giontec became more articulate;[33] it is located on the right Adige not far from a part of the valley where the Adige river created a swamp. South of the modern village of Salorno/Salurn an extensive necropolis (1st–4th century AD) was on the left bank of Adige (fig. 2). The graves were presumably aligned along a road parallel to the river. Most of the tombs were from the 2nd century AD, as witnessed by the coins recovered inside them.[34]

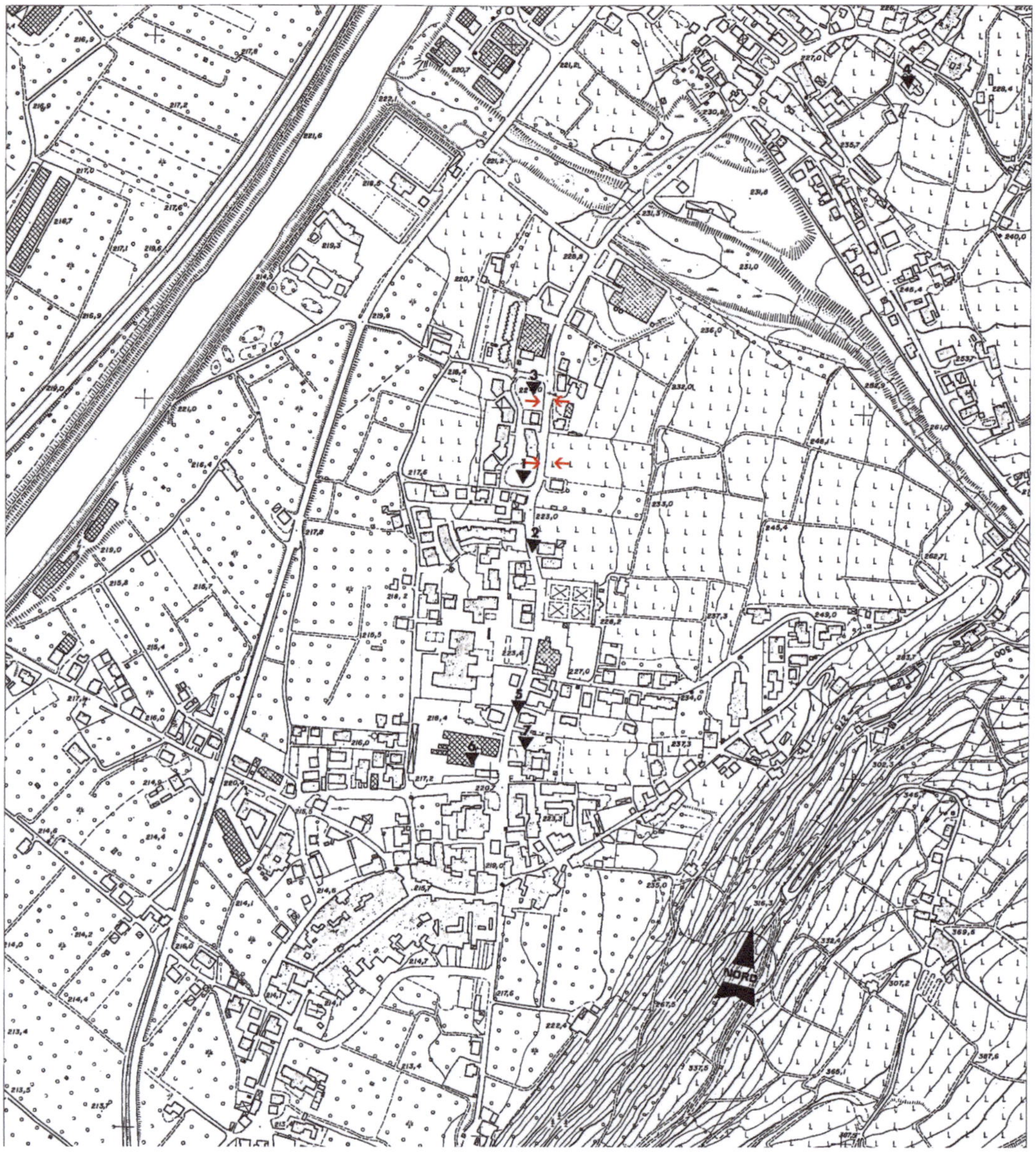

Fig. 3: The area of Egna-Khan.

The territory would seem to become progressively more functional to the needs of the *limes*, as it is probably shown by an inscription recovered in *Tridentum* that recalls the activity of an important man, *Gaius Valerius Marianus* (end 2nd century AD – 3rd century AD).[35] This region suffered a period of crisis in the 3rd century AD, generally related to the arrival of Alemanni. Military control over this territory could have been strengthened. Moreover, the impact of a destructive earthquake seems to have added to the political and economic crisis.[36]

Fig. 4: The stele found in Villa/Vill.

The archaeological data of Laghetti /Laag seem to suggest a change of use during the 4th century AD, due to the abundant presence of *militaria*, in the valleys closely linked to the Adige, prestigious residences were created.[37] In 357 AD Constance II passes from *Tridentum* to reach the Danube *limes*.[38] The pressure of the Goths of Alaric (402 AD) and of the Ostrogoths of Radagaisus (405 AD) seems to have determined a situation of instability, but not the end of the settlement organization along the course of the Adige.

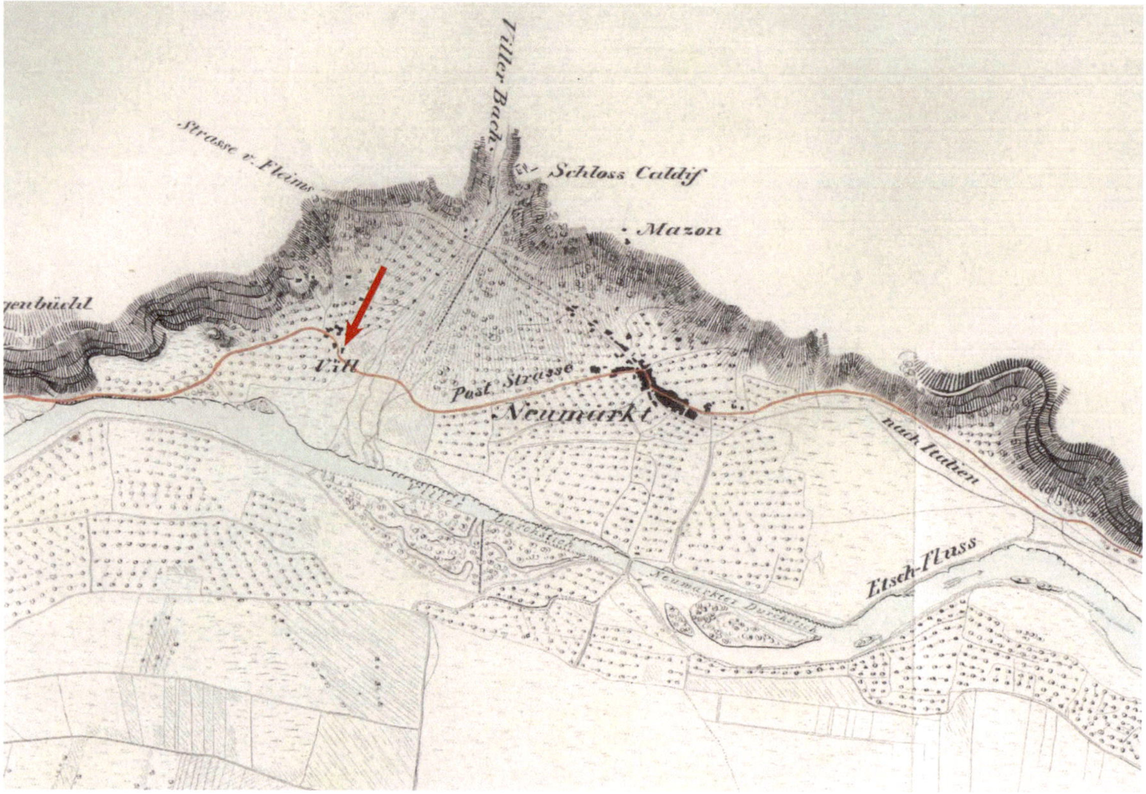

Fig. 5: Location of the area of Villa/Vill.

Economy and Activities Connected with the Settlement

We do not have written sources on productive activities along the Adige Valley, but it is possible to reconstruct the local economy through various data. There must have certainly been a trade in food (especially milk derivates and meat too), but it is difficult to recognize their trade system because they must have been kept in wooden or wicker containers. Through the ethnographic tradition we can imagine that the flow of wood along the course of the Adige could have been practiced and that, perhaps, as attested from the Middle Ages onwards, saw mills should have been present where the streams entered the Adige.[39] A Roman relief of *Attis* found in Trento could be connected with a *collegium* of *dendrophoroi*.[40]

The wool craftsmanship had to be widespread, as attested by the loom weights dated back in Roman age spread throughout the territory. Through ethnographic tradition we can imagine flocks of sheep that passed along the Adige valley from the Alps to the plain and vice versa.

Most of the houses were built with local stones and wood. One of the main activities was to work with the stone, practiced above all in *Tridentum*, where ancient quarries on the eastern hills are attested. Many artefacts were created in Roman times (from the 1st century BC onwards) in local stones ("Marble of Pilo "or "Rosso di Trento"): small altars; sarcophagi, columns, capitals, but also slabs, polygonal blocks for paving roads and for milestones. In the upper part of the Adige Valley the porphyry had to be worked; it was used to create small grain mills.[41]

We know that *tegulae* with the stamp *AVRESIS* and variants[42] are widespread throughout the Adige river. This stamp was found in contexts dating back to the early Imperial age: for example, in *Tridentum* at "*porta Veronensis*" dated, in the current state of research, in the age of Claudius, and in another building, in a context dated back between the age of Augustus and the Flavian age.[43] A large sorting warehouse of these artefacts was seen in Ora/Auer area (Unterberg/Sottomonte) in the first half of the 20th century, but the kilns have not yet found, although many clues seem to identify the Ora/Auer as a production center.[44] As the stamp appears in buildings that seem connected to central power ("*porta Veronensis*" in *Tridentum*) or in buildings connected with roads and drainage works (for example, the building identified as a road station in Egna Khan and the one of Laives/Leifers – San Giacomo/ St. Jakob) we could here hypothesize a production of *tegulae* controlled by the central power.

The stamp *Caius Rutilius* (with variants) is also well documented. The most ancient specimens appear in a building of Laives/Leifers San Giacomo/St. Jakob dated in the first half of the 1st century AD. The findings of tiles-bearing this stamp are mainly concentrated in the area between Verona and the modern town of Bolzano.[45] It is perhaps possible to hypothesize that brick products of *gens Critonia* arrived as far as Adige Valley from the workshops located in the district of Ravenna or in the Padua area.[46] From the north Adriatic area came the brick tiles with the stamp *Pansiana* widespread from the mid-1st century AD to 79 AD.[47]

A workshop of clay products (tiles and loom weights) was located at higher altitude, as that one in Prà de Rover near Cei in Val Lagarina (4th–5th century AD), south of *Tridentum*[48]. In Prà de Rover (about 900 m over sea level) there were clay pits, the possibility of water supply, large areas for processing and timber for baking ovens. North of *Tridentum*, in Cortaccia/Kurtatsch and in Predonico along a side street that becomes more and more important in Late Antiquity, some kilns have been identified but, at the current state of research, no stamp can be associated without doubt. In Cortaccia/Kurtatsch stamps with three circles have also been identified.

Conclusions

Numerous data suggest that River Adige influenced the organization of the settlement and the productive landscape of the district. If we examine the distribution of pre-Roman and Roman sites placed in the Adige Valley, it becomes clear that many sites were located along the river and that the presence of marshes and the danger of damage caused by floods forced the choice of conoids as settlement sites. It is also evident that many sites were placed in control of the river and of the valley, as river and valley, if on the one hand facilitated the possibility of trade, on the other hand represented a dangerous location.

The plantations are supposed to be mainly relegated to hilly slopes or to a few areas of the valley floor sheltered from floods, instead of expanding upon the whole valley, as nowadays. Consequently, in the Roman era a large part of the Adige Valley, is supposed to have had a typical vegetation of a wet environment; only sites protected from the river floods could be used for agricultural practices. In fact, stone presses for grapes have been noticed in the hilly area facing the Adige Valley (for example in Cortaccia/Kurtatsch).

The presence of the urban center of *Tridentum* linked to the river, the attestation of Roman stations on the valley floor, the settlement continuity of several sites along the river, the presence of Roman coins and of people who choose iconographic motifs typical of the Roman world in their stelae, the trade of terra sigillata and of other goods from the Mediterranean area, the circulation of heavy tiles that contributed to the creation of new buildings, they are all elements that make us realize that the river, with the road-system, must have been an aggregating element in the territory.

Notes

[1] From north to south: Adige Valley from the area of the modern center of Merano/Meran as far as the southern outskirts of Trento and Val Lagarina as far as the area of the modern town of Rovereto.

[2] About morphodynamics, see Angelucci 2016.

[3] See the "carta Claricini" dated between 1845–1850, probably in 1847 (Ranzi – Werth 2016).

[4] Battisti 2010, 11.

[5] Marzatico et al. 2010, 283.

[6] Marzatico et al. 2010, 283.

[7] Nicolis 2010.

[8] Zanforli – Tecchiati 2010, 615 f. with previous bibliography; see also Alberti 2015.

[9] The remarkable findings of amphorae coming from the Aegean area (end of 6th century – beginning of the 4th century BC) carried out at Forcello near *Mantua* (De Marinis 1987, 213) led to the hypothesis that the wine was decanted into wooden containers (Sassatelli 1987, 89 f.), most suitable for mixed transport (waterways and paths) up to the innermost places: see Dal Ri – Rizzi 2005, 200–203. Olive oil was carried too.

[10] See now Alberti 2015, with previous bibliography.

[11] Marzoli – Wiel Marin 2016, 306–314. Cups from the district of Attica (1st half of the 4th century BC) were found there.

[12] Gorini 2000, 208; Marzoli et al. 2016, 209.

[13] Zanforlin 2010, 591 (Laives/Leifers); Coltorti 1991, 24 (Vadena /Pfatten).

[14] Hor. Carm, 4, 4, 17–18; 4,14. Strabo, who wrote the Geographia by 18 AD, says that the populations in the Alpine region seem to change following the Augustan conquest, as they were forced to pay taxes and were controlled directly by the central power (Strabo 4.6.9 C 207).

[15] Buonopane 2000, 160- 166.

[16] Marzatico – Endrizzi 2016, 160–162; Marzoli et al. 2016, 208.

[17] Clemente – Mosca 2015, 683. See also Steidl 2011.

[18] CIL V, 8003; CIL V, 5050.

[19] Marcone 1991, passim.

[20] Bassi 2016, 175–178. 190.

[21] Faoro 2014, 99- 103. 116.

[22] Ciurletti 2014, 21–24 (proposal for the reconstruction of the urban scheme, without a port). However, the identification of a river port is generally problematic (see Chevallier 1968, 90). For the location and the function of two river docks in Trento in the Middle Ages, see Mosca 2009, 460.

[23] About the origin of the *Quadragesima Galliarum*: De Laet 1949, 170; France 1993, 895–927. *Publicum Portorium* already existed starting from the Republican age; it was then reorganized in the age of Augustus, until in the 2nd century (with Traianus or Adrianus) the management of the *portorium* was passed by *societates* to private *conductores*; Marcus Aurelius had reaffirmed imperial control over customs entrusting them to *procuratores* (De Laet 1949, 384–388. 403–405).

[24] CIL V, 5090 = ILS 1561 = IBR 68 (dated back in 217 or 246 AD); another inscription, even if less clear, would appear to be connected to the *statio*: see Buchi, 2000, 91 f. In *statio Miensis* in the 3rd century AD the *Quadragesima Galliarum* was required, that is to say the tax of one fortieth of the value of the commodity. The tax was due for goods coming from Gauls, but later also from Germany. Here we can suppose that *stationes* occupied larger area than what was usually considered until now.

[25] CIL V, 5079 = IBR 57 (*Isis Augusta*); CIL V, 5080 = ILS 1859 = IBR 58 (*Isis Myrionyma*); CIL V5081 = ILS 3160 = IBR 59 (a slave *Mercurialis* works as *vilicus*). These inscriptions seem to date back in the late 2nd century AD: see Buchi 2000, 91.

[26] Marzoli et al. 2016, 209.

[27] Marzoli et al. 2016, 211.

[28] Marzoli et al. 2016, 212: in the necropolis so far identified, most of the artefacts date back to the late Roman empire.

[29] Marzoli – Rizzi 2005.

[30] Di Stefano 2002.

[31] Dal Ri – Fusi 1997, 94–104.

[32] Paci 2002, 146 f.; Alberti 2002.

[33] Bassetti et al. 2004, 330.

[34] The excavations had been carried out at the end of the 19th century; the data were published in the 20th century (Noll 1963).

[35] CIL V, 5036 = ILS 5016 (end 2nd century AD/ 3rd century AD; see Buchi 2000, 81–83). This man was a *patronus* of *Tridentum*. Probably he was in charge of the procurements of the *legio III Italica* (established in 165–166 AD) allocated to the *Castra Regina* (Regensburg); or he was responsible for collecting the tax (*annona*) intended to maintain the *legio III Italica*.

[36] The building-*statio* of *Endidae* was destroyed by an earthquake in the 3rd century AD: see Galli- Galadini 2002.

[37] Marzoli et al. 2015.

[38] Amm XVI, 10- 20.

[39] A production plant operating by water, connected to the presence of running water, has been identified e.g. in Mezzocorona-Giontec (Bassetti et al. 2004, 330). However, it could also be connected to a smith workshop or be multi-functional.

[40] Mosca 2011, 440–444.

[41] Mosca 2015.

[42] Five types are known: see Bassi et al. 2005, 154–157.

[43] Bassi et al. 2005, 155. But we can think that the production has continued ever further, as it would seem to be demonstrable in relation to the presence of olive oil amphorae Dressel 20 (1st–3rd century AD).

[44] Bassi et al. 2005, 157.

[45] Buchi 1979, 154, n. 12; Bassi 1995, 88–92; Bassi et al. 2005, 156; Righini 2008, 362 f.

[46] Zerbinati 1993, 113.

[47] Buonopane 2000, 160; about the origin and the diffusion see Matijasic 1983, 993–995.

[48] Rigotti 2007, 94 f. fig. 44; 174 fig. 129.

Image Credits

Fig. 1: Steidl 2011; elaboration by A. Mosca. – Fig. 2: Noll 1963; elaboration by A. Mosca. – Fig. 3: Di Stefano 2002, 161 fig. 3; elaboration by A. Mosca. – Fig. 4: Paci 2002. – Fig. 5: Ranzi – Werth 2016; elaboration by A. Mosca.

References

Alberti 2002

A. Alberti, Rinvenimenti romani e medievali da Villa di Egna, in: Dal Ri – Di Stefano 2002, 338–345.

Alberti 2015

A. Alberti, Il ripostiglio di Vadena, in: G. Kaufmann (ed.), Archeologia dell'Oltradige/ Archäologie des Überetsch (Innsbruck 2015) 611–644.

Angelucci 2016

D. E. Angelucci, La Valle dell'Adige: genesi e modificazione di una grande valle alpina come interazione tra dinamiche naturali e fattori antropici, in: V. Rovigo (ed.), Il fiume, le terre, l'immaginario: l'Adige come fenomeno storiografico complesso. Memorie Accademia Roveretana degli Agiati 4 (Rovereto 2016) 9–43.

Bassetti et al. 2004

M. Bassetti – M. Bersani – G. Dalmeri – N. Degasperi – E. Mottes – F. Nicolis, Montagna e Valle dell'Adige tra preistoria e storia. Primi dati delle recenti indagini dell'Ufficio Beni Archeologici, in: M. De Vos (ed.), Archeologia del territorio, metodi, materiali, prospettive, Medjerda e Adige: due territori a confronto (Trento 2004) 317–365.

Bassi 2016
C. Bassi, Tridentum città romana. Osservazioni cronologiche sulla fondazione, in: S. Solano (ed.), Dai Camunni ai Romani: archeologia e storia della romanizzazione alpina. Atti del Convegno Breno-Cividate Camuno 2013 (Rome 2016) 175–195.

Bassi et al. 2005
C. Bassi – L. Dal Ri – C. Marzoli – S. Di Stefano, Sviluppo economico del territorio del municipium di Tridentum nella prima età imperiale. Il caso del bollo figulino AVRESIS, in: G. Ciurletti – N. Pisu (eds.), I territori della via Claudia Augusta. Incontri di archeologia (Trento 2005) 151–163.

Battisti 2010
M. Battisti, L'antica età del Bronzo in Vallagarina, in: Dal Ri et al. 2010, 1–36.

Buchi 1979
E. Buchi, La produzione laterizia dell'agro veronese e del Trentino meridionale in età romana, in: Congresso sulla romanità del Trentino e di zone limitrofe, Atti Accademia Agiati Rovereto s. 6,19 (Trento 1979) 135–170.

Buchi 2000
E. Buchi, Dalla colonizzazione della Cisalpina alla colonia di Tridentum, in: E. Buchi (ed.), Storia del Trentino 2 (Bologna 2000) 47–131.

Buonopane 2000
A.Buonopane, Società, economia, religione, in: E. Buchi (ed.), Storia del Trentino 2 (Bologna 2000) 133–239.

Chevallier 1968
R. Chevallier, Problems de Topographie historique posés par l'étude d'un bassin fluvial dans l'antiquité, in: Actes du quatre onzième congrès national des societés Savantes, Rennes 1966 (Paris 1968) 71–98.

Ciurletti 2014
G. Ciurletti, Prima della Torre di Piazza: la porta Veronensis, in: La Torre di Piazza nella storia di Trento. Funzioni, simboli, immagini, Atti della giornata di studio Trento 2012 (Trento 2014) 19–40.

Clemente – Mosca 2015
G. Clemente – A. Mosca, Tra Alpi e Danubio: l'unità difficile di un territorio conteso (IV–V secolo d.C.), in: Culti e religiosità nelle province danubiane, Atti del II Convegno Internazionale Ferrara novembre 2013 (Bologna 2015) 683–716.

Dal Ri – Fusi 1997
L. Dal Ri – G. Fusi, Archeologia nel comune di Egna e nelle zone adiacenti, in: H. Gritsch (ed.), Egna Alto Adige-Sudtirolo. Nel passato e nel presente (Egna 1997) 69–99.

Dal Ri – Di Stefano 2002
L. Dal Ri – S. Di Stefano (eds.), Archaeologie der Roemerzeit in Siidtirol, Archeologia romana in Alto Adige. Beni culturali in Alto Adige 1 (Bolzano 2002).

Dal Ri – Rizzi 2005
L. Dal Ri – G. Rizzi, Strade dell'età del Ferro nella conca di Bressanone, in: Atti Accademia Rovertana Agiati 8, 2 (Rovereto 2005) 199–229.

Dal Ri et al. 2010

L. Dal Ri – P. Gamper – H. Steiner (eds.), Abitati dell'età del Bronzo e del Ferro. Controllo delle vie di comunicazione attraverso le Alpi, Beni culturali in Alto Adige/Studi e ricerche 6 (Trento 2010).

De Laet 1949

D. J. De Laet, Portorium, étude sur l'organisation douaniére chez les Romains, surtout à l'epoque du Haut Empire (Bruges 1949).

De Marinis 1986

R. C. De Marinis, Le anfore greche da trasporto, in: R.C. De Marinis (ed.), Gli Etruschi a nord del Po (Mantova 1986) 211–224.

Di Stefano 2002

S. Di Stefano, La struttura romana di Egna-Kahn, in: Dal Ri – Di Stefano 2002, 158–259.

Faoro 2014

D. Faoro, M. Appuleius Sex. Filius, legatus. Augusto, Tridentum e le Alpi orientali, Aevum 88 (2014) 99–124.

France 1993

J. France, Quadragesima Galliarum, L' organisation douanière des provinces alpestres gauloises et germaniques de l'Empire romain (Ier siècle avant J.C. – IIIe siècle après J.C.), MEFRA 105, 1993, 895–927.

Galli – Galadini 2002

P. Galli – F. Galadini, Analisi paleosismologiche nel sito di Egna: tracce di un antico terremoto distruttivo, in: Dal Ri – Di Stefano 2002, 301–317.

Gorini 2000

G. Gorini, Presenze monetali e tesaurizzazione, in: E. Buchi (ed.), Storia del Trentino 2 (Bologna 2000) 241–285.

Marcone 1991

A. Marcone, La frontiera del Danubio tra strategia e politica, in: A. Schiavone (ed.), Storia di Roma 2,2 (Torino 1991) 469–490.

Marzatico et al. 2010

F. Marzatico – N. Degasperi – L. Moser – S. Zamboni, Aspetti del paesaggio insediativo in Trentino fra l'età del Bronzo e l'età del Ferro, in: Dal Ri et al. 2010, 277–296.

Marzatico – Endrizzi 2016

F. Marzatico – L. Endrizzi, Dalla protostoria alla storia: Reti e Romani alla luce delle fonti archeologiche, in: S. Solano (ed.), Dai Camunni ai Romani: archeologia e storia della romanizzazione alpina, Atti del Convegno Breno-Cividate Camuno 2013 (Rome 2016) 147–173.

Marzoli et al. 2015

C. Marzoli – G. Bombonato – A. De Leo, Die römerzeitliche Besiedlung von St. Pauls, in: G. Kaufmann (ed.), Archeologia dell'Oltradige/Archäologie des Überetsch (Innsbruck 2015) 151–168.

Marzoli et al. 2016

C. Marzoli – A. De Leo – S. Di Stefano, La romanizzazione in area media alpina atesina. Dinamismo e conservatorismo culturale in una terra di confine, in: S. Solano (ed.), Dai Camunni ai Romani:

archeologia e storia della romanizzazione alpina, Atti del Convegno Breno-Cividate Camuno 2013 (Rome 2016) 207–220.

Marzoli – Wiel Marin 2016
C. Marzoli – F. Wiel Marin, Siebeneich/Settequerce, Tutela dei Beni Culturali in Alto Adige / Denkmalpflege in Südtirol 2012–2013, 2016, 306–314.

Matijasic 1983
R. Matijasic, Cronografia dei bolli laterizi della figulina Pansiana nelle regioni adriatiche, MEFRA 95, 1983, 961–995.

Mosca 2011
A. Mosca, Le vie del legno in area alpina centro orientale in età romana e medievale. Documentazione archeologica e aspetti topografici, Archivio per l'Alto Adige 104–105, 2011, 425–444.

Mosca 2015
A. Mosca, Marble and Stones Used in Central Eastern Alpine Area and in Northern Area of Benacus: Topographical Reconstruction of Trade Routes and Aspects of Use in the Roman Era, in: P. Pensabene – E. Gasparini (eds.), Interdisciplinary Studies on Ancient Stones ASMOSIA X, Rome, May 2012 (Rome 2015) 574–584.

Nicolis 2010
F. Nicolis, Il Dosson di Faedo nella Valle dell'Adige, Trento, in: Dal Ri – Gamper – Steiner 2010, 299–305.

Noll 1963
R. Noll, Das römerzietliche Gräberfeld von Salurn (Innsbruck 1963).

Paci 2002
G. Paci, Stele romane decorate dell'Alto Adige, in: Dal Ri – Di Stefano 2002, 136–149.

Ranzi – Werth 2016
R. Ranzi – K. Werth, Il fiume Adige da Merano a Borghetto nelle carte di Leopoldo de Claricini 1847 (Trento 2016).

Righini 2008
V. Righini, Bolli laterizi nelle vallate alpine, in: P. Basso – E.Buchi, (eds.), Est enim ille flos Italiae... Vita economica e sociale nella Cisalpina romana, Verona, 30 novembre, 1 dicembre 2006 (Verona 2008) 361–368.

Rigotti 2007
A. Rigotti, Lagarina romana. Storia antica e archeologia del territorio dal II secolo a.C. al V secolo d.C. (Rovereto 2007).

Sassatelli 1987
G. Sassatelli, La situazione in Etruria padana, in Crise et transformation des sociétés archaiques de l'Italie antique au V siécle avant J.C. Actes de la table ronde organisée par l'école Française Rome et l'unité de recherches etrusco-italiques associé au CMRS (UA 132) 19–21 novembre 1987, Collection de l'école Française de Rome 137, 51–100.

Steidl 2011
B. Steidl, Zum Grenzverlauf zwischen Noricum. Raetien und der Regio X im Eisacktal, Bayerische Vorgeschichtsblätter 76 (München 2011) 157–176.

Zanforlin 2010
L. Zanforlin, Il sito protostorico di via Galizia a Laives/Leifers (prov. Di Bolzano), in: Dal Ri – Gamper – Steiner 2010, 571–595.

Zanforlin – Tecchiati 2010
L. Zanforlin – U. Tecchiati, Topografia archeologica della Bassa Atesina (prov. di Bolzano), in: Dal Ri et al. 2010, 597–619.

Zerbinati 1993
E. Zerbinati, Note per un dossier sui bolli laterizi scoperti ad Adria e nel Polesine, in: C. Zaccaria (ed.), I laterizi di età romana nell'area nordadriatica (Rome 1993) 93–126.

L'impatto delle alluvioni sullo sviluppo urbano ed economico della città di Parma, alla luce dei recenti rinvenimenti dallo scavo di via del Conservatorio

Anna Rita Marchi – Ilaria Serchia

Lo scavo di un ampio settore urbano della città romana di Parma, a pochi metri dall'omonimo torrente, ha permesso l'indagine stratigrafica di più eventi alluvionali che hanno, fin dalle origini, condizionato lo sviluppo urbano della colonia di diritto romano, fondata nel 183 a.C. (fig. 1). La città di Parma si trova nella parte occidentale della pianura padana, in Emilia Romagna, ed è attraversata dall'omonimo torrente che nasce dal monte Marmagna, negli Appennini, e scorre sulla destra idrografica del fiume Po, nel quale confluisce dopo 92 km di percorso. Si tratta di un corso d'acqua dal carattere torrentizio, in secca per gran parte dell'estate e soggetto a piene impetuose nelle stagioni più piovose. Le indagini archeologiche effettuate a fasi alterne, tra il 2005 e il 2016,[1] hanno portato in luce una serie di elementi utili alla comprensione del complesso rapporto tra l'insediamento umano e il corso d'acqua, che ha condizionato in maniera determinante la crescita, lo sviluppo e l'involuzione di questo territorio fin dall'età del Ferro.

Prima della romanizzazione il paesaggio di pianura si presentava diverso rispetto a quanto documentato nei secoli successivi. Fino a questo momento l'intervento umano sul territorio non aveva agito profondamente, in particolare la pianura era caratterizzata dall'alternarsi di zone di pascolo e zone agricole, intervallate da boschi paludosi e corsi d'acqua non messi a regime. L'intervento di Roma sul paesaggio di pianura, oltre a segnarlo attraverso la fondazione di colonie con valenza militare, politica ed economica, si esplica con la riorganizzazione agricola del territorio anche attraverso massicce operazioni di sistemazione idraulica con la creazione di vie e canali secondo la pendenza dei suoli. Non è corretto però ritenere che in epoche precedenti non esistessero per nulla forme di organizzazione territoriale, tracce delle quali sono state ampiamente documentate, in indagini archeologiche più o meno recenti,[2] per tutto il territorio parmense di pianura. Sono proprio i fenomeni alluvionali e di impaludamento che in alcuni casi hanno cancellato le tracce di queste prime sistemazioni, in particolare in tutte quelle aree più esposte per motivi geologici e naturali. [3]

Nell'età del Ferro i primi insediamenti del parmense sono documentati in forma sparsa nel territorio, nel quale in apparenza manca un unico centro propulsore: i villaggi individuati, sono distribuiti lungo le principali direttrici di comunicazione naturale, il Parma, il Baganza, l'Enza e il Taro.[4] In questo periodo la sistemazione territoriale si concretizza attraverso la costruzione di canali e infrastrutture specifiche, come vasche per la raccolta delle acquae e pozzi, che non costituiscono elementi di grande impatto ambientale. Fino a tempi recenti si riteneva, in base ai rinvenimenti archeologici, che questi nuclei insediativi, pienamente strutturati nel VI secolo a.C., fossero distribuiti

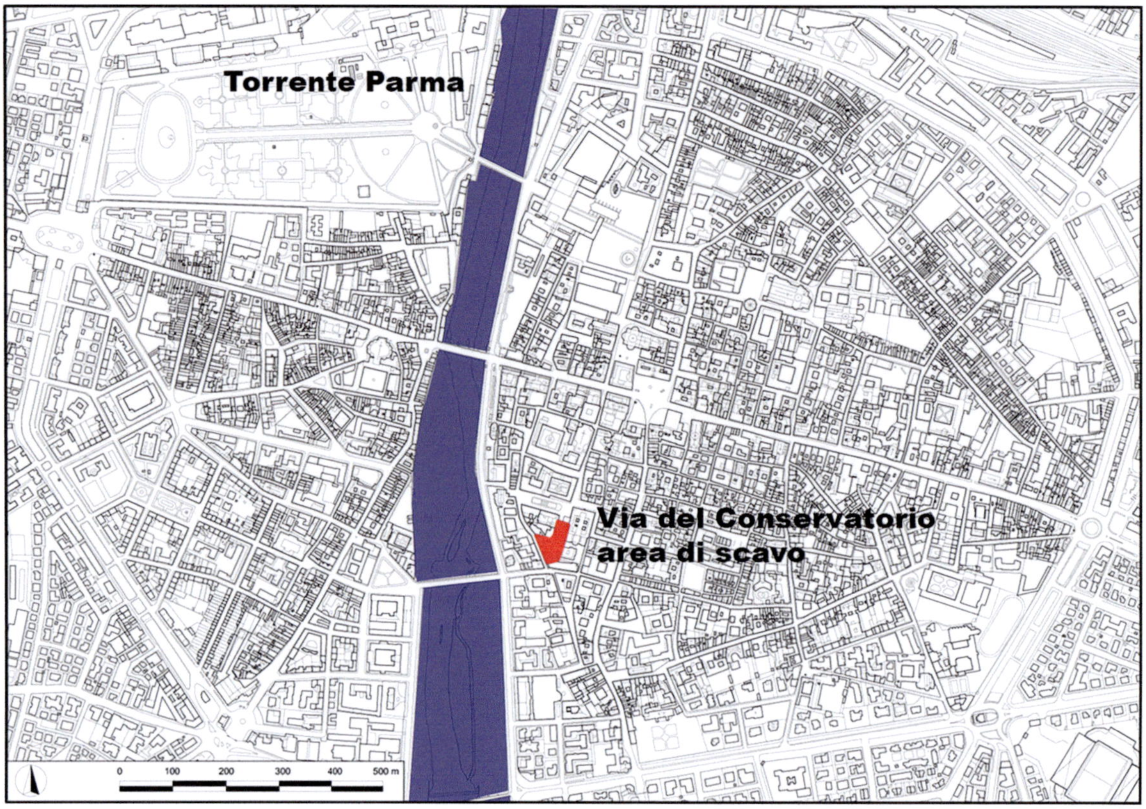

Fig. 1: Pianta del centro storico di Parma con il posizionamento dell'area di scavo prossima al corso del torrente.

esclusivamente attorno alla città attuale mentre le recenti scoperte di via del Conservatorio, all'interno del centro storico di Parma, hanno permesso di ampliare le conoscenze sul popolamento del territorio. Anche in questo caso è determinante nella scelta del luogo la vicinanza a un corso d'acqua, il torrente Parma. Sono state riportate in luce tracce di frequentazione risalenti al V–IV secolo a.C., conservate esclusivamente in negativo nel terreno, a causa di fenomeni di dilavamento e successiva sovrapposizione delle strutture di età romana.

Questi eventi hanno causato la quasi completa asportazione del piano di vita dell'epoca, ricostruibile esclusivamente attraverso brevi residui di suolo. Sono state indagate buche di palo, pertinenti ad almeno due unità abitative, distribuite intorno a un pozzo con camicia in ciottoli, e ambienti accessori, probabilmente un piccolo magazzino, oltre a buche di scarico, dalle quali è stato recuperato materiale ceramico databile tra il V e il IV secolo a.C., fra cui ciotole in ceramica depurata a bande di probabile produzione locale (fig. 2). Tuttavia il reperto che denota una maggiore antichità è un fondo di *kylix* di importazione attica, forse a figure nere, che attesterebbe l'inizio della frequentazione di Parma almeno attorno al 500 a.C. e confermerebbe scambi commerciali con la Grecia, sicuramente attraverso la città di Spina. Il dato è particolarmente rilevante se

Fig. 2: Ceramica etrusco-padana dalla scavo di via del Conservatorio a Parma.

contestualizzato alla recessione nella quale sembrano invece cadere, in base alle attuali conoscenze, gli altri centri del territorio,[5] dove risulta scarsa la presenza di ceramica depurata, così detta etrusco-padana[6], e di ceramica attica a figure rosse.

L'insediamento di via del Conservatorio, pur mantenendo tracce di frequentazione fino al IV secolo a.C., sembrerebbe poi rapidamente abbandonato a causa di un evento alluvionale che di fatto ha anche alterato in maniera decisiva la conformazione del suolo. L'area rimase poi disabitata fino alla fondazione della colonia romana nel II secolo a.C. La colonia romana, fondata nel 183 a.C. si estendeva a sud fino al limite meridionale dell'area di scavo, proprio dove sono stati ritrovati i resti della cinta muraria di età repubblicana, mentre a ovest arrivava a lambire la sponda del torrente.[7]

L'imponente struttura difensiva era orientata est-ovest, si conservava per 5 m di lunghezza e per circa 1 m in elevato, comprensivo delle fondazioni, e misurava 3 m di spessore. In corrispondenza della terminazione orientale si ammorsava a un altro segmento murario, probabilmente parte di una porta urbica, aggettante per 1,50 m verso l'interno della città (fig. 3). Al muro, fondato a una quota di -4,10 m dall'attuale piano di calpestio, si appoggiava, lungo il prospetto interno nord, un terrapieno documentato da un residuale strato limo-argilloso pulito, come già documentato nelle mura repubblicane di Piacenza.[8]

I due segmenti murari erano costruiti interamente in mattoni legati ad argilla, disposti, per l'intero spessore del muro, su filari orizzontali, affiancati per il lato corto e poggiati su una platea di fondazione con cornice basale leggermente aggettante rispetto allo spiccato del muro. L'elevato era composto da mattoni interi che misuravano 53 × 35 cm con uno spessore di 4,5 cm, rinvenuti in alcuni casi frammentari a causa degli assestamenti strutturali post deposizionali. In fondazione gli stessi elementi laterizi, frammentati, erano disposti in maniera caotica su un piano uniforme non rifinito esteriormente.[9]

Su questo versante cittadino l'apparato difensivo era completato da una palizzata in legno con catene, rimasta in uso per un breve periodo di tempo, che inoltre proteggeva la città dalle frequenti esondazioni del torrente. In età repubblicana, il corso d'acqua svolgeva quindi una duplice funzione: come naturale barriera difensiva del settore occidentale della città e come fonte di approvvigionamento diretto di risorse idriche.

Fig. 3: Tratto delle mura repubblicane di Parma rinvenute nello scavo di via del Conservatorio.

In questo settore urbano già nel II sec. a.C. sono documentati impianti per la produzione di ceramica. Nell'isolato trovarono posto almeno due fornaci a pettine, prossime a una bottega, costruita in legno, con tornio a piede caratterizzato da un disco rotante superiore su un perno di sostegno verticale infisso a terra attraverso un disco inferiore, il volano, spinto con i piedi. La scelta del luogo di produzione non sembra essere casuale, la vicinanza del fiume rappresentava indubbiamente una risorsa.

Nel 43 a.C., durante le guerre per il principato, Parma si schierò con Ottaviano e per questo fu posta sotto assedio e saccheggiata da Antonio. A seguito della vittoria di Ottaviano la colonia fu rifondata come *Iulia Augusta Parmensis.* Nello stesso periodo fu oggetto di un profondo rinnovamento urbanistico che portò l'abitato a espandersi oltre le mura repubblicane e anche oltre le opere provvisionali di contenimento delle acque del torrente, probabilmente in questo periodo messe a regime. Nell'isolato sud-occidentale furono costruite, sugli impianti per la produzione di ceramica, almeno due *domus*, una delle quali pavimentata a mosaico, con ambienti riscaldati, e con pareti decorate da intonaci dipinti. Le *domus* affacciavano, a oriente, su un asse stradale basolato attraverso un portico su colonne (fig. 4). Il nuovo quartiere residenziale di età imperiale è stato sommerso più volte da alluvioni, sempre però ripristinato, attraverso ristrutturazioni che portarono al rialzamento dei piani di vita interni.

Nel II sec. d.C. non si riscontra più il fervore edilizio del secolo precedente a causa di periodi alterni di crisi economica, anche se i rinvenimenti archeologici

Fig. 4: Resti delle *domus* di età imperiale dallo scavo di via del Conservatorio a Parma.

documentano continuità dell'attività edificatoria a Parma, o perlomeno interventi di manutenzione e restauro degli edifici pubblici. Negli scavi condotti da Mirella Marini Calvani, nella zona sud-occidentale della città romana, è stato recuperato un grande architrave a girali floreali di età traianea (98–117 d.C.) e frammenti architettonici decorati ad astragali, perle e dentelli, datati tra Adriano e gli Antonini riutilizzati in tempi successivi nelle difese spondali.[10] Questi reperti sono, secondo Manuela Catarsi, forse riferibili a un tempio di Minerva che doveva sorgere nell'area dell'attuale Palazzo del Tribunale di Parma,[11] confinante a est con la nostra area di scavo.

La città subì nel III secolo d.C. la pressione esercitata dal passaggio di Jutungi e Alemanni in pianura padana, ricordato nel 270 d.C. Nello stesso periodo l'isolato sud-occidentale tornò a essere considerato marginale all'impianto urbano come in età repubblicana. Uno strato a matrice limosa con molti frammenti di intonaco dipinto è stato rinvenuto tra il portico delle *domus* e la via basolata, disteso a coprire le fondazioni dei pilastri del portico e la crepidine stradale, ma non l'asse stradale. Dopo il susseguirsi delle alluvioni di I e II secolo d.C., che comportarono continui ripristini e restauri degli edifici pubblici e privati, gli eventi esondativi del III secolo d.C. non furono più prontamente fronteggiati, a causa delle mutate condizioni politiche ed economiche nelle quali versava la città.

Fig. 5: Resti dei magazzini di IV–V secolo d.C. dallo scavo di via del Conservatorio a Parma.

Fig. 6: Tratto delle mura tardoantiche di Parma, dallo scavo di via del Conservatorio.

Solo a partire dal IV secolo d.C., sotto l'imperatore Costantino, si riaccese l'attività edificatoria, in condizioni sociali profondamente mutate, che portarono alla trasformazione di interi settori cittadini, soprattutto periferici ai centri della piena età imperiale. Nella seconda metà dello stesso secolo, in via del Conservatorio, fu ulteriormente innalzato il piano di vita, posto al di sopra di un esteso riporto alluvionale che copriva le *domus* augustee, le fondazioni delle quali furono parzialmente riutilizzate nella costruzione di un edificio, composto da almeno undici vani, utilizzato per lo stoccaggio e la conservazione delle merci. Questo evento fu suggellato da un rito propiziatorio con la deposizione di una falce di ferro, due bicchieri/lucerna in vetro e un mattone spezzato.[12] Il magazzino rimase in uso fino al repentino abbandono avvenuto tra il V e il VI secolo, quando una forte alluvione provocò lo spostamento del torrente, che da questo momento cominciò a scorrere decisamente più a est rispetto all'alveo documentato per tutta l'epoca romana. Questo evento rese necessaria la costruzione di nuove difese spondali, costituite da due muri ortogonali tra loro e disposti all'incrocio di un cardine e di un decumano della città romana (fig. 5).

Il muro est/ovest, legato ad angolo retto al muro nord-sud, al momento della scoperta, si presentava in buone condizioni di conservazione; è stato indagato per una lunghezza complessiva di 16 m, aveva spessore di 4 m e si conservava in elevato fino a più di 3,00m. L'imponente struttura era realizzata in muratura piena di mattoni e malta. I mattoni, "tipo" *sesquipedali,* erano messi in opera interi e raramente spezzati, e misuravano cm 44 × 32 × 9, misure che si avvicinano al tipico mattone di tradizione romana, differendo in maniera significativa solo nello spessore. I paramenti esterni della struttura presentavano un'apparecchiatura piuttosto regolare, dove i mattoni, disposti a cadenza alternata per il lato lungo e per quello corto, componevano l'elevato, che si impostava su una fondazione gradinata, caratterizzata però dall'andamento ondulato dei corsi di posa (fig. 6).

Fig. 7: Tratto delle difese spondali di età tardoantica dallo scavo di via del Conservatorio a Parma.

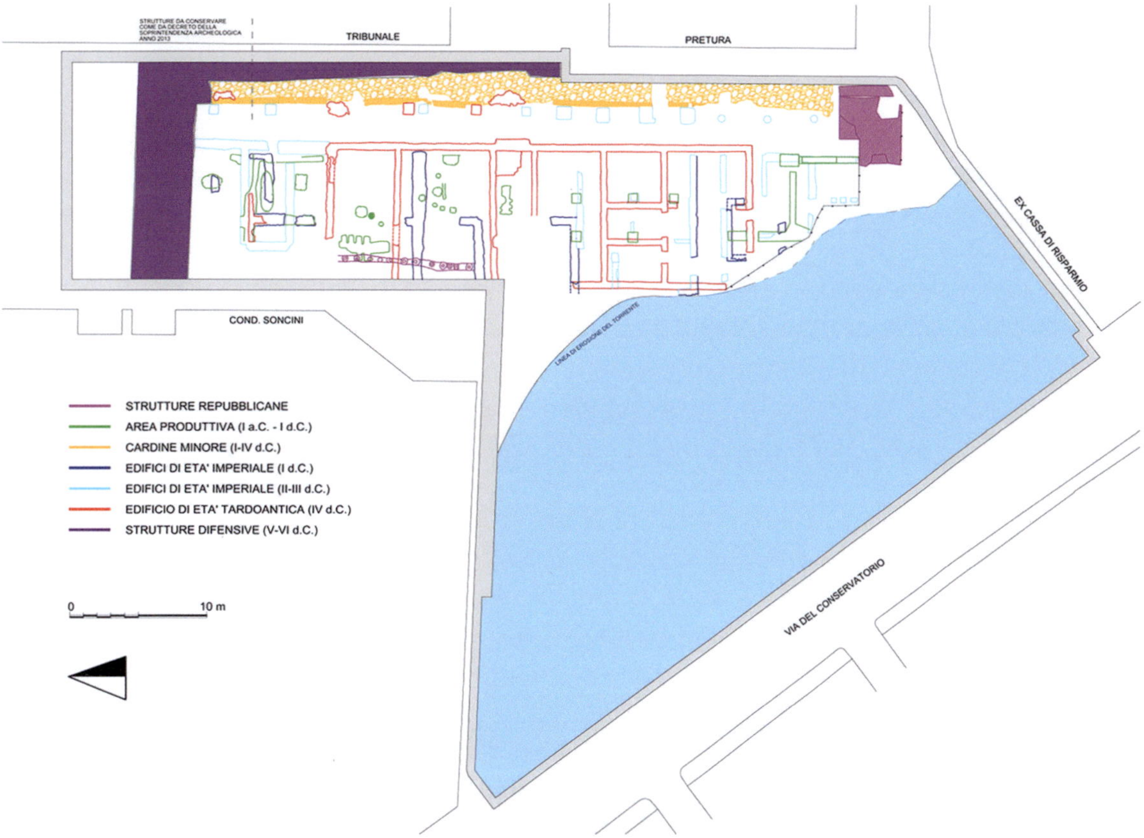

Fig. 8: Tavola diacronica dei rinvenimenti di via del Conservatorio dall'età del Ferro all'epoca tardoantica in relazione al corso del torrente Parma.

Il muro nord/sud era messo in opera con la medesima tecnica e con l'utilizzo degli stessi materiali, ma nel nucleo erano impiegati anche ciottoli disposti di taglio, poggiava inoltre direttamente sui resti di una via basolata di età imperiale, riutilizzata come basamento di fondazione. Al momento della scoperta si sono rilevate però condizioni ben diverse di conservazione rispetto al muro est/ovest; infatti il setto nord/sud era stato completamente *spoliato* in antico dei mattoni lungo il prospetto ovest[13] (fig. 7). Il settore sud-occidentale dell'insediamento di età imperiale, fino al momento della costruzione delle mura di VI secolo totalmente incluso all'interno del perimetro urbano,[14] fu di fatto tagliato fuori dall'abitato, con un sensibile restringimento della città[15] (fig. 8). La zona fu in seguito sporadicamente frequentata, come attestato dalla presenza di un modesto sepolcreto, datato al VI–VII secolo, impostato sui livelli di crollo dei magazzini di età tardo antica.[16]

Anche durante il medioevo l'area continuò a essere soggetta a frequenti fenomeni alluvionali, intervallati da brevi periodi di stasi, nei quali comunque la zona rimase disabitata. La pressione del torrente lungo il fianco occidentale della città di Parma è documentata anche dalla presenza di altri ampi resti di muraglioni di difesa spondale rinvenuti lungo la direttrice nord-sud.[17] Del resto questa zona della città è ricordata cinta di mura nel testamento della regina Cunegonda, della prima metà del IX secolo, nel quale sono citati il monastero di Sant'Alessandro e quello di San Bartolomeo, entrambi *infra muras civitate Parmensis.*[18] Nell'alto medioevo il fiume continuò a scorrere nell'alveo orientale, come anche archeologicamente riscontrato nello scavo di via del Conservatorio, dove le ghiaie fluviali sono emerse lungo il limite di scavo ovest a una profondità di 3,56 m dal piano di vita attuale. Solo dalla seconda metà del XII secolo, a causa di un'altra epocale alluvione, ricordata dalle fonti nel 1177,[19] il fiume tornò a scorrere più a ovest, dove era anche in età romana. La città tornò quindi a espandersi in questo settore: nel XIII secolo con la costruzione di modeste abitazioni, trasformate in seguito, nel XV–XVI secolo, in sontuosi palazzi signorili.

Note

[1] Lo scavo è stato diretto dalla Soprintendenza Archeologica dell'Emilia Romagna con il finanziamento della Gespar S.p.A. di Parma e condotto dalla ditta Gea s.r.l. "Ricerca e Documentazione Archeologica".

[2] Locatelli et al. 2013.

[3] Rottoli 2009, 32–35.

[4] I principali rinvenimenti di insediamenti dell'età del Ferro nel parmense sono a Pontetaro, San Pancrazio, in via Cremonese, Baganzola, Cortile San Martino, Pedrignano, Casalora di Ravadese, Casalbaroncolo, Beneceto, San Lazzaro, via Saragat, via Formenti, via Casalunga, Strada Bassa dei Folli, via Traversetolo, via Felice da Mareto, Gaione, Quartiere Cinghio Sud e via Guidorossi, trattati nell'insieme in Locatelli et al. 2013.

[5] Locatelli 2013, 10–13.

[6] Casini et al. 1986, 246–265; De Marinis 1986, 140–163; Cattani et al. 1988, 11–19; Chiaramonte Trerè 2009; Buoite 2013, 23–26.

[7] Livio pone la colonia di Parma "in agro qui proxime Boiorum ante Tuscorum fuerat", Historiarum (Ab Urbe Condita) 39. 55, 6–8.

[8] Locatelli 2015, 155.

[9] Marchi – Serchia c.s.

[10] Marini Calvani 2001, 68 s. fig. 136.

[11] Catarsi 2009b, 430.

[12] Marchi – Serchia 2018, 91–93.

[13] In base al materiale rinvenuto all'interno degli scassi più profondi operati nel muro, è possibile datare le spoliazioni al XIV–XV secolo.

[14] Catarsi 2009a, 397 s. Carta 26.

[15] Allo stato attuale delle indagini non è possibile collegare direttamente a Teodorico la costruzione delle mura tardoantiche di Parma, anche se esistono diverse notizie che legano il nome del re goto alla città (Cassiodoro, Var., 8, 29–30). Sulle fortificazioni dei Goti in Italia si veda: Settia 1993, 101–131; Brogiolo – Gelichi 1996, 11–24.

[16] Marchi – Serchia 2017, 79–88.
[17] Ampi tratti di mura a difesa dalle acque del torrente sono stati messi in luce negli scavi di P.le Paër, del golfo mistico del Teatro Regio, del palazzo dell'Agricoltura, di via dell'Università, di strada al Ponte Caprazucca e di Borgo Salnitrara.
[18] Per una lettura critica del testamento di Cunegonda si veda La Ferla 1981, 7 e note 47. 48.
[19] Chronicon Parmense, 5–7.

Indice delle figure

Fig. 1: rielaborazione dell'autore. – Fig. 2: immagine originale Ilaria Serchia. – Fig. 3–8: © documentazione di scavo.

Bibliografia

Brogiolo – Gelichi 1996
G. P. Brogiolo – S. Gelichi, I castra tardoantichi (quarta metà del VI secolo), in: Nuove ricerche sui castelli altomedievali in Italia settentrionale (Firenze 1996) 11–24.
Buoite 2013
C. Buoite, Produzione e distribuzione della ceramica nell'Emilia occidentale in età arcaica, in: Locatelli et al. 2013, 23–26.
Butzer 2008
K. W. Butzer, Challenges for a Cross-disciplinary Geoarchaeology: The Intersection between Environmental History and Geomorphology, Geomorphology 101, 2008, 402–411. <http://sites.utexas.edu/butzer/files/2017/03/Butzer-2008-Challenges4cross-disciplinarygeoarchaeology.pdf> (19th August 2019)
Casini et al. 1986
S. Casini – P. Frontini – E. Gatti, La ceramica fine, in: Gli Etruschi a nord del Po. Catalogo della mostra 1 (Mantova 1986) 246–265.
Catarsi 2009a
M. Catarsi, La forma urbis, in: Vera 2009, 397 s.
Catarsi 2009b
M. Catarsi, Architettura religiosa, in: Vera 2009, 430.
Cattani et al. 1988
M. Cattani – F. Ferri – A. Losi, Classificazione della ceramica dell'età del Ferro. La ceramica depurata, in: Modena dalle origini all'anno mille. Studi di archeologia e storia. Catalogo della Mostra 2 (Modena 1988) 11–19.
Chiaramonte Trerè 2009
C. Chiaramonte Trerè (ed.), Archeologia preromana in Emilia occidentale. La ricerca oggi tra monti e pianura, Atti della giornata di Studi, Milano 2006 (Milano 2009).

Chronicon Parmense 1902
G. Bonazzi (ed.), Chronicon Parmense: ab anno MXXXVIII usque ad annum MCCCXXXVIII, RIS 11 2(Città di Castello 1902).
De Marinis 1986
R. De Marinis, L'abitato etrusco del Forcello di Bagnalo San Vito, in: Gli Etruschi a nord del Po, Catalogo della mostra, I (Mantova 1986) 140–163.
La Ferla 1981
G. La Ferla, Parma nei secoli IX e X: «civitas» e «suburbium», in: Storia della città 18 (Parma 1981) 5–32.
Locatelli 2013
D. Locatelli, Vivere in un villaggio dell'età del Ferro. Villaggi e occupazione del territorio nell'area di Parma, in: Locatelli et al. 2013, 10–13.
Locatelli et al. 2013
D. Locatelli – L. Malnati – D. F. Maras (eds.), Storie della prima Parma. Etruschi, Galli, Romani: la origini della città alla luce delle nuove scoperte archeologiche. Catalogo della mostra, Museo Archeologico Nazionale di Parma, Palazzo della Pilotta, 12 gennaio–2 giugno 2013 (Roma 2013).
Locatelli 2015
D. Locatelli, Le mura di Piacenza, in: L. Malnati- V. Manzelli (eds.), Brixia. Roma e le genti del Po. Un incontro di culture. III–I secolo a.C., Catalogo della mostra- Brescia 9/5/2015- 17/1/2016 (Firenze 2015) 155.
Marchi – Serchia 2017
A. R. Marchi – I. Serchia, Il sepolcreto tardoantico con tracce di celebrazione del pasto funebre dallo scavo di via del Conservatorio a Parma, Temporis Signa 11, 2016, CISAM (Spoleto 2017) 79–88.
Marchi – Serchia 2018
A. R. Marchi – I. Serchia, La stipe votiva di Parma, via del Conservatorio, in: S. Gelichi – C. Cavallari – M. Medica (eds.), Medioevo svelato. Storie dell'Emilia Romagna attraverso l'archeologia (Cremona 2018) 91–93.
Marchi – Serchia c. s.
A. R. Marchi – I. Serchia, Parma, via del Conservatorio. La scoperta e lo scavo di un tratto delle mura di difesa di II secolo a.C., in: J. Bonetto – E. Bukowiecki – R. Volpe (eds.), Alle origini del laterizio romano – Nascita e diffusione del mattone cotto nel Mediterraneo tra IV e I sec. a.C., Convegno Internazionale, Padova 26–28 aprile 2016 (in corso di stampa).
Marchi et al. c. s.
A. R. Marchi – M. Matteazzi – I. Serchia, Il sistema di smaltimento delle acque a Parma in epoca romana: nuovi dati dallo scavo di via del Conservatorio, in: Antichità Alto Adriatiche (in corso di stampa).
Marini Calvani 2001
M. Marini Calvani (ed.), Guida al Museo Archeologico Nazionale di Parma (Ravenna 2001).
Rottoli 2009
M. Rottoli, L'ambiente antico, in: Vera 2009, 17–41.

Settia 1993
A. A. Settia, Le fortificazioni dei goti in Italia, in: Teodorico il Grande e i Goti in Italia, Atti del 13 Congresso Internazionale di Studi sull'Alto Medioevo – Milano 1992 (Spoleto 1993) 101–131.

Vera 2009
D. Vera (ed.), Storia di Parma 2: Parma Romana (Parma 2009).

Printing and Binding
Books on Demand GmbH
In de Tarpen 42, 22848 Norderstedt, Germany